On the Mystery Dramas
THE PORTAL OF INITIATION
and
THE SOUL'S PROBATION

by
Rudolf Steiner

THE ANTHROPOSOPHIC PRESS

These three lectures were published in German by Rudolf Steiner Verlag in the volume entitled, *Über die Mysteriendramen, Drei Vorträge*. They were translated for this volume by Ruth Pusch. The quotations from Rudolf Steiner's dramas are from *Four Mystery Dramas*, translated by Ruth and Hans Pusch, and are used by kind permission of Steiner Book Centre, Vancouver, Canada.

ISBN 0-88010-060-5

Cover design by Peter van Oordt

Cover photograph of the *Portal of Initiation*, Scene 4,
stage of the Goetheanum, Dornach, Switzerland

*

Dedicated to the memory of
HANS PUSCH
whose efforts and devotion
brought about the performances of
Rudolf Steiner's four Mystery Dramas
for three decades here in America
and also—with these performances—
the English translation of the dramas.

*

Table of Contents

I

Self-Knowledge as Portrayed in the
Rosicrucian Mystery,
The Portal of Initiation

Many of you know that recently in Munich we repeated last year's performance of Schuré's drama, *The Children of Lucifer*. We also put our efforts into the production of a Rosicrucian Mystery in which we tried in a variety of ways to bring to expression what is living in our movement. For one thing, it was meant to show how the life of anthroposophy and its impulses can flow into art, into artistic form. Besides that, we should be aware that this Rosicrucian Mystery contains many of our spiritual scientific teachings that perhaps only in future years will be discerned. Please do not misunderstand me when I say that if people would exert themselves to some degree to read what is in it—not between the lines but right in the words themselves, though certainly in a spiritual sense— if people would exert themselves during the next few years to try to work with the drama, I would not have to give any more lectures for a long time. Much could be discovered in it that otherwise I would have to put forth as one or another theme in lectures. It is much more practical, however, to do this together as a group rather than as single individuals. It is fortunate in one sense that everything that lives in spiritual science also exists in such a form.

In relation to the Rosicrucian Mystery I should today like to speak about certain peculiarities of human self-knowledge. For this we will have to remind ourselves how the individuality living in the body of Johannes Thomasius brings about a characterization of himself. Therefore, I wish to start my lecture with a recitation of the scenes from the Rosicrucian Mystery that portray the self-knowledge of Johannes.

*

SCENE TWO

A place in the open; rocks and springs. The whole surroundings are to be thought of as within the soul of Johannes Thomasius. What follows is the content of his meditation.

(From the springs and rocks resounds:)
O man, know thou thyself.

Johannes   For many years these words
          of weighty meaning I have heard.
          They sound to me from air and water;
          they echo up from depths of earth.
          And just as in the acorn secretly
          the structure of the mighty oak is pressed,
          within the power of these words
          there is contained
          all that my thought can comprehend
          about the nature of the elements,
          of souls as well as spirits,
          of time and of eternity.
          The world and my own nature
          are living in the words:
          O man, know thou thyself!

(From the springs and rocks resounds:)
O man, know thou thyself.

And now!—within me
it is becoming terribly alive.
Around me darkness weaves,
within me blackness yawns;
out of the world of darkness it resounds,
out of soul-blackness it rings forth:—
O man, know thou thyself!

(There sounds from springs and rocks:)
O man, know thou thyself.

And now it robs me of myself.
I change with every hour of the day.
I melt into the night.
The earth I follow in her cosmic course.
I rumble in the thunder,
I flash within the lightning,
I am.—But oh, I feel
already separated from my being.
I see my body's shell.
It is an alien being outside myself;
it is remote from me.
There hovers nearer now another body
and with its mouth I have to speak:
'He brought me bitter sorrow;
I gave him all my trust.
He left me in my grief alone.
He robbed me of the warmth of life
and thrust me deep into cold earth.'
She, whom I left, unhappy one,
I was now she herself,
and I must suffer her despair.

3

Self-knowledge lent me strength
to pour myself into another self.
O cruel words!
Your light is quenched by its own power.
O man, know thou thyself!

(There sounds from springs and rocks:)
O man, know thou thyself.

You guide me back again
into the spheres of my own being.
Yet how do I behold myself!
My human form is lost;
as raging dragon I must see myself,
begot of lust and greed.
I clearly sense
how an illusion's cloud
has hid from me till now
my own appalling form.
The fierceness of my being will devour me.
And running like consuming fire
through all my veins I feel those words,
which hitherto with elemental power
revealed to me the truth of suns and earths.
They live within my pulse,
they beat within my heart,
and even in my thought itself I feel
those unfamiliar worlds flare up as wild
        desires.
This is the fruitage of the words:
O man, know thou thyself.

(There sounds from springs and rocks:)
O man, know thou thyself.

4

There from the dark abyss,
what being gloats on me?
I feel the chains
that hold me fettered fast to you.
Prometheus was not chained so fast
upon the cliffs of Caucasus
as I am chained to you.
Who are you, horrifying being?

(There sounds from springs and rocks:)
O man, know thou thyself.

Oh, now I recognize you.
It is myself.
So knowledge chains to you, pernicious
    monster,

(Maria enters, but is not noticed
by Johannes for the time being)

me, myself, pernicious monster.
I sought to flee from you.
The worlds wherein my folly fled,
in order to be free from my own self,
have dazzled and have blinded me.
And blind I am once more within the
    blinded soul.
O man, know thou thyself!

(There sounds from springs and rocks:)
O man, know thou thyself.

Johannes   *(as if coming to himself, sees Maria. The*
           meditation passes over into inner reality.)
           Maria, you are here!

Maria   I've looked for you, my friend,
although I know
how dear to you is solitude,
now that so many people's views
have flooded through your soul.
And I know, too, that at this time
my presence cannot help my friend.
An urge that is obscure
is driving me to you this very moment
when words of Benedictus have called up,
instead of light, such bitter grief
out of your spirit depths.

Johannes How dear to me is solitude!
How often have I sought it out,
to find in it myself,
whenever pain and joy of men have driven me
into the labyrinths of thought.
Maria, that is past.
What Benedictus' words at first
drew forth out of my soul,
and what I then lived through
from everything those people said,
seems little to me now
if I compare it to the storm
which solitude has brought
into my heavy brooding.
O this solitude!
It drove me into cosmic spaces;
it tore me from myself.
Within that being to whom I brought such
    grief
I rose again but as another,
and had to bear the pain
which I myself had caused.
The fierce, dark solitude

6

then gave me back myself
but only to appal me
at the abyss of my own being.
— — — — — — — —

For me, man's final refuge,
for me, my solitude is lost.

Maria   I must repeat my words to you:
no one but Benedictus can now help you.
The firm support we lack,
we both must have from him.
For know, I also can no longer bear
the riddle of my life,
unless some sign from him
can make the answer clear to me.
The lofty wisdom, pointing out
that only semblance and illusion
are spread out over all our life
as long as human thinking grasps alone its
      surface,
I've often held it up before my mind.
And every time it says:
you must be clear that an illusion
is shrouding you, though often it may seem
      the truth:
that evil fruit could come from your desire
to wake that light in others
which lives in you yourself.
My soul's best part can see
that heavy feelings of oppression
in you, my friend,
from living at my side
are too a portion of the thorny path
that leads you to the light of truth.
You must live through each terror

7

to which illusion can give birth
before the truth reveals itself to you:
thus speaks your star.
Yet through this starry word is also clear to me
that we must wander on the spirit paths
    together.
But when I seek these paths,
there spreads itself before my gaze dark night.
And blacker still becomes this night
through much which I must meet
as fruit of my own being.
We both must look for clarity in that light,
which for the eye can vanish
but never be extinguished.

Johannes   Maria, are you then aware
through what my soul has fought its way?
A heavy load indeed
has fallen upon you, dear friend.
Yet foreign to your being is that power
which has so wholly shattered me.
You can ascend to brightest heights of truth;
you can direct your steady gaze
at men's confusion.
In light, in darkness,
you will affirm yourself.
But every moment can
deprive me of myself.
I had to plunge into those people
who through their words revealed themselves
    just now.
I followed one into the cloister's loneliness,
I heard within the other's soul
Felicia's tales.
I was each one,
but for myself I died.

I'd have to have the faith
that beings spring from nothingness,
if I should cherish any hope
that from the nothingness in me
a human being ever could be born.
They force me out of fear into the darkness,
and hunt me through the darkness into fear,
these words imbued with wisdom:
O man, know thou thyself!

(From the springs and rocks resounds:)
O man, know thou thyself.

SCENE NINE

The same place as in Scene Two.

(From rocks and springs resounds:)
O man, unfold your being.

Johannes O man, unfold your being!
For three years now I've sought
for power of soul, with wings of courage,
to give these words their truth.
Through them a man who frees himself can
    conquer,
and conquering himself, can find his freedom.
O man, unfold your being!

(From rocks and springs resounds:)
O man, unfold your being.

This power of soul is rising from within me
but only gently touching spirit hearing.
It harbours in itself the hope

9

that, growing, it will lead the human spirit
from narrowness far out to distant worlds,
just as the tiny acorn
mysteriously can expand
into the giant body of the noble oak.
The spirit in itself can bring to life
what weaves in air and water,
what has condensed to earth beneath.
For man can grasp
what has been taking hold of life
within the elements, in souls and spirits,
in time and in eternity.
The whole world-being lives within my soul,
when in the spirit there has taken root
the power that gives these words their truth:
O man, unfold your being!

(From rocks and springs resounds:)
O man, unfold your being.

I feel them sounding in my soul,
rousing themselves to give me strength.
There lives in me the light,
there speaks around me brightness,
there germinates in me the light of soul,
there works in me world-radiance.
O man, unfold your being!

(From rocks and springs resounds:)
O man, unfold your being.

I find myself secure on every side,
wherever these words' power follows me.
It will illuminate for me the senses' darkness
and will uphold me in the spirit heights.

It will enfill me with soul-substance
throughout all course of time.
The essence of the world I feel in me
and I must find myself in every world.
I see the being of my soul enlivened
through power that is my own.
I rest within myself.
I gaze on rocks and springs;
they speak the very language of my soul.
I find myself again within that being
to whom I brought such bitter grief,
and out of her I call out to myself:
'Oh, you must find me once again
and ease my suffering.'
The spirit's light will give me strength
to live the other self within myself.
O words of hope,
you stream forth power to me from all the
      worlds:
O man, unfold your being.

(From rocks and springs resounds:)
O man, unfold your being.

You let me feel my weakness
and place me close to lofty aims of gods,
and blissfully I feel
such lofty aims' creative might
within my frail earth form.
Out of myself shall be revealed the purpose
for which the seed lies hidden in me.
And to the world I'll give myself
by living out my very being.
I want to feel these words' full power,
although they sound so gently.
They shall become for me a quickening fire

11

in my soul forces
and on my spirit paths.
I feel now how my thinking penetrates
deep hidden grounds of worlds
and how its radiant light illumines them.
Such is the germinating power of these words:
O man, unfold your being.

(From rocks and springs resounds:)
O man, unfold your being.

From light-filled heights a Being shines on me,
and wings I feel
that lift me up to him.
I too will free myself, as every being does
who overcomes himself.

(From rocks and springs resounds:)
O man, unfold your being.

I see that Being.
I shall become like him in future times.
The spirit will then free itself in me
through you, exalted goal of man.
I will now follow you.

(Maria enters)
My eye of soul has been awakened
by spirit beings who have welcomed me.
And as I gaze into the worlds of spirit,
I feel within myself that power:
O man, unfold your being.

(From rocks and springs resounds:)
O man, unfold your being.

Maria, you are here?

Maria   My soul has led me here.
I could behold your star:
it shines in its full power.

Johannes   I can unfold that power from within me.

Maria   So closely are we linked
that your soul's life
lets its light shine into my soul.

Johannes   Maria, you are then aware
of what has just revealed itself?
For me, man's core of confidence,
for me, the certainty of being has been won.
I feel indeed the power of the words
which everywhere can guide me:
O man, unfold your being!

(From rocks and springs resound:)
O man, unfold your being.

In these scenes two levels of development, two steps in the unfolding of our souls, are shown.

Now please do not find it strange when I say that I do not mind interpreting this Rosicrucian Mystery just as I have interpreted other pieces of literature in our group. What I have often said about other poetry can also be brought before our souls in a lively, spontaneous way by this drama. In fact, I have never failed to point out that a flower knows little, indeed, of what someone who is looking at it will find in it; yet, whatever he finds *is* contained

13

in it. And in speaking about *Faust*, I explained that the poet did not necessarily know or feel everything in the words he was writing down that later would be discovered in them. I can assure you that nothing of what afterward I could say about the Rosicrucian Mystery, and that I know now is in it, was in my conscious mind as I wrote down the various scenes. The scene-pictures grew one by one, just like the leaves of a plant. One cannot bring forth a character by first having an idea and then turning this into a concrete figure. It was continually interesting to me how each scene grew out of the others preceding it. Friends who knew the earlier parts said that it was remarkable how everything came about quite differently from what one could have imagined.

This Mystery Drama exists now as a picture of human evolution in the development of a single person. I want to emphasize that true feeling makes it impossible to throw a cloak of abstractions around oneself in order to present anthroposophy; every human soul is different from every other and, at its core, must be different, because each one undergoes the experience of his own development. For this reason, instruction to the many can provide only general directions. One can give the complete truth only by applying it to a single human soul, to a soul that reveals its human individuality in all its uniqueness. If, therefore, anyone should consider the figure of Johannes Thomasius in such a way as to transfer the specific description of that figure to general theories of human development, it would be absolutely incorrect. If he believed that he would experience exactly what Johannes Thomasius experienced, he would be quite mistaken. For while in the widest sense what Johannes Thomasius had to undergo is valid for everyone, in order to have the same specific experiences one would have to *be* Johannes Thomasius. Each person is a "Johannes Thomasius" in his own fashion.

Everything in the drama is presented, therefore, in a completely individual way. Through this, the truth portrayed by the particular figures brings out as clearly as possible the development of the soul of a human being. At the beginning, Thomasius is shown in the physical world, but certain soul-happenings are hinted at that provide a wide basis for such development, particularly an experience at a somewhat earlier time when he deserted a girl who had been lovingly devoted to him. Such things do take place, but this individual happening has a different effect on a man who has resolved to undertake his own development. There is one deep truth necessary for him who wants to undergo development: self-knowledge cannot be achieved by brooding within oneself but only through diving into the being of others. Through self-knowledge we must learn that we have emerged from the cosmos. Only when we give ourselves up can we change into another Self. First of all, we are transformed into whatever was close to us in life.

When at first Johannes sinks more deeply into himself and then plunges in self-knowledge into another person, into the one to whom he has brought bitter pain, we see this as an example of the experience of oneself within another, a descent into self-knowledge. Theoretically, one can say that if we wish to know the blossom, we must plunge into the blossom, and the best method of acquiring self-knowledge is to plunge again, but in a different way, into happenings we once took part in. As long as we remain in ourselves, we experience only superficially whatever takes place. In contrast to true self-knowledge, what we think of other persons is then mere abstraction.

For Thomasius at first, what other people have lived through becomes a part of him. One of them, Capesius, describes some of his experiences; we can observe that they are rooted in real life. But Thomasius takes in more. He is listening. His listening is singular; later, in Scene

Eight, we will be able to characterize it. It is really as if Thomasius' ordinary Self were not present. Another deeper force appears, as though Thomasius were creeping into the soul of Capesius and were taking part in what is happening from there. That is why it is so absolutely important for Thomasius to be estranged from himself. Tearing the Self out of oneself and entering into another is part and parcel of self-knowledge. It is noteworthy, therefore, that what he has listened to in Scene One, Thomasius says, reveals:

> . . . A mirrored image of the whole of life,
> that showed me clearly to myself.
> What is revealed to us out of the spirit
> has led me to perceive how many men,
> who think themselves a whole, in fact
> bear in themselves one single facet only.
> In order to unite within myself
> all these divergent sides,
> I started boldly on the path taught here—
> and it has made of me a nothing.

Why has it made a "nothing" of him? Because through self-knowledge he has plunged into these other persons. Brooding in your own inner self makes you proud, conceited. True self-knowledge leads, first of all, by having to plunge into a strange Self, into suffering. In Scene One Johannes follows each person so strongly that when he listens to Capesius he becomes aware of the words of Felicia within the other soul. He follows Strader into the loneliness of the cloister, but at first this has the character of something theoretical. He cannot reach as far as he is later led, in Scene Two, through pain. Self-knowledge is deepened by the meditation within his inner Self. What was shown in Scene One is shown changed in Scene Two through self-knowledge intensified from abstraction to a

16

concrete imagination. Those well-known words, which we have heard through the centuries as the motif of the Delphic Oracle, bring about a new life for this man Johannes, though at first it is a life of estrangement from himself.

Johannes enters, as a knower-of-himself, into all the outer phenomena. He finds his life in the air and water, in the rocks and springs, but not in himself. All the words that we can let sound on stage only from outside are actually the words of his meditation. As soon as the curtain rises, we have to confront these words, which would sound louder to anyone through self-knowledge than we can dare to produce on the stage. Thereafter, he who is learning to know himself dives into the other beings and elements and thus learns to know them. Then in a terrible form the same experience he has had earlier appears to him.

It is a deep truth that self-knowledge, when it progresses in the way we have characterized, leads us to see ourselves quite differently from the way we ever saw ourselves before. It teaches us to perceive our "I" as a strange being.

Man believes his own outer physical sheath to be the closest thing to himself. Nowadays, when he cuts a finger, he is much more connected with the painful finger than when, for instance, a friend hurts him with an unjust opinion. How much more does it hurt a modern person to cut his finger than to hear an unjust opinion! Yet he is only cutting into his bodily sheath. To feel our body as a tool, however, will come about only through self-knowledge.

Whenever a person grasps an object, he can feel his hand to some degree as a tool. This, too, he can learn to feel with one or another part of his brain. The inward feeling of his brain as instrument comes about at a certain level of self-knowledge. Specific places within the brain are localized. If we hammer a nail, we know we are doing it with a tool. We know that we are also using as tool one or another part of the brain. Through the fact that these things are objective and can become separate and strange to us, we come to know our brain as something quite separate from us. Self-knowledge requires this sort of objectivity as regards our body; gradually our outer sheath becomes as objective to us as the ordinary tools we use. Then, as soon as we have made a start at feeling our bodily sheath as separate object, we truly begin to live in the outside world.

Because a person feels only his body, he is not clear about the boundary between the air outside and the air in his lungs. All the same, he will say that it is the same air, outside and inside. So it is with everything, with the blood, with everything that belongs to the body. But what belongs to the body cannot be outside and inside— that is mere illusion. It is only through the fact that we allow the internal bodily nature to become outward that in truth it finds a further life out in the rest of the world and the cosmos.

In the first scene recited today there was an effort to express the pain of feeling estranged from oneself—the pain of feeling estranged because of being outside and within all the other things. Johannes Thomasius' own bodily sheath seems like a person outside himself. But just because of that—that he feels his own body outside—he can see the approach of another body, that of the young girl he once deserted. It comes toward him; he has learned how to speak with the very words of the other being. She says to him, whose Self has widened out to her:

He brought me bitter sorrow;
I gave him all my trust.
He left me in my grief alone.

18

He robbed me of the warmth of life
and thrust me deep into cold earth.

Then guilt, very much alive, rises up in the soul when, plunging our own Self into another and attaching ourselves to the pain of this other being, the pain is spoken out. This is a deepening, an intensifying. Johannes is truly *within* the pain, because he has caused it. He feels himself dissolving into it and then waking up again. What is he actually experiencing?

When we try to put all this together, we will find that the ordinary, normal human being undergoes something similar only in the condition we call kamaloka. The initiate, however, has to experience in this world what the normal person experiences in the spiritual world. Within the physical body he must go through what ordinarily is experienced outside the physical body. All the elements of kamaloka have to be undergone as the elements of initiation. Just as Johannes dives into the soul to whom he has brought such grief, so must the normal human being in kamaloka dive into the souls to which he has brought pain. It is just as if a slap in the face has to come back to him; he has to feel the same pain. The only difference is that the initiate experiences this in the physical body, and other people after death. The one who goes through this here will afterward live otherwise in kamaloka. But even all that one undergoes in kamaloka can be so experienced that one does not become entirely free. It is a most difficult task to become completely free. A man feels as if he were chained to his physical conditions.

In our time one of the most important elements for our development—not yet so much in the Greco-Roman epoch but especially important nowadays—is that the human being must experience how infinitely difficult it is to become free of himself. Therefore, a notable initiation experience is described by Johannes as feeling chained to

19

his own lower nature; his own being seems to be a creature to which he is firmly fettered:

I feel the chains
that hold me fettered fast to you.
Prometheus was not chained so fast
upon the cliffs of Caucasus
as I am chained to you.

This belongs to self-knowledge; it is a secret of self-knowledge. We should try to understand it correctly.

A question about this secret could be phrased like this: have we in some way become better human beings by becoming earth dwellers, by entering into our physical sheaths, or would we be better by remaining in our inner natures and throwing off those sheaths? Superficial people, taking a look at life in the spirit, may well ask: why ever do we have to plunge down into a physical body? It would be much easier to stay up there and not get into the whole miserable business of earthly existence.

For what reason have the wise powers of destiny thrust us down here? Perhaps it helps our feelings a little to say that for millions and millions of years the divine, spiritual powers have worked on the physical body. Because of this, we should make more out of ourselves than we have the strength to do. Our inner forces are not enough. We cannot yet be what the gods have intended for us if we wish to be only what is in our inner nature, if our outer sheaths do not work some corrections in us. Life shows us that here on earth man is put into his physical sheaths and that these have been prepared for him by the beings of three world epochs. Man has now to develop his inner nature. Between birth and death he is bad; in Devachan he is a better creature, taken up by divine, spiritual beings who shower him with their own forces. Later on, in the Vulcan epoch, he will be a perfect being. Now on the earth he is a being who gives way to this or that desire. Our hearts, for one thing, are created with such wisdom that they can hold out for decades against the excesses we indulge in, such as drinking coffee. What man can be today through his own will is the way he travels through kamaloka. There he has to learn what he can be through his own will, and that is certainly nothing very good. Whenever man is asked to describe himself, he cannot use the adjective "beautiful." He has to describe himself as Johannes does in Scene Two:

Yet how do I behold myself!
My human form is lost;
as raging dragon I must see myself,
begot of lust and greed.
I clearly sense
how an illusion's cloud
has hid from me till now
my own appalling form.

Our inner nature stretches flexibly within our bodily sheaths and is hidden from us. When we approach initiation, we learn really to see ourselves as a kind of raging dragon. Therefore, these words are drawn up out of the deepest perception; they are words of self-knowledge, not of self-brooding:

It is myself.
So knowledge chains to you, pernicious monster,
me myself, pernicious monster.

At bottom they are both the same, one the subject, the other the object.

I sought to flee from you.

This flight, however, merely leads the human being directly to himself.

But then the crowd turns up, the crowd we find ourselves in when we really look into ourselves. We find

21

ourselves to be a collection of lusts and passions we had not noticed earlier, because each time we wanted to look into ourselves our eyes were distracted to the world outside. Indeed, compared to what we would have seen inside, the world outside is wonderfully beautiful. Out there, in the illusion, in the maya of life, we stop looking at ourselves inwardly. When people around us, however, begin to talk all kinds of stupidity and we cannot stand it, we escape to where we can be alone. This is quite important at some levels of development. We can and should collect ourselves; it is a good means of self-knowledge. But it can happen that, coming into a crowd of people, we can no longer be alone; those others appear, either within us or outside us, no matter; they do not allow us to be alone. Then comes the experience we must have: solitude actually brings forth the worst kind of fellowship.

For me, man's final refuge,
for me, my solitude is lost.

Those are genuine experiences. Do not let the strength, the intensity, of the happenings trouble you. You do not have to believe that such strength and intensity as described must necessarily lead to anxiety or fear. It should not prevent anyone from also plunging into these waters. No one will experience all this as swiftly or with such vehemence as Johannes does; it had to come about for him in this way for a definite purpose, even prematurely, too. A normal self-development proceeds differently. Therefore, what occurs in Johannes so tumultuously must be understood as an individual happening. Because he is this particular individual, who has suffered a kind of shipwreck, everything he undergoes takes place much more tempestuously than it otherwise would. He is confronted by the laws of self-development in such a way that they throw him completely off balance. As for us, one thing should be awakened by this description of

22

Johannes, that is, the perception that true self-knowledge has nothing to do with trite phrases, that true self-knowledge inevitably leads us into pain and sorrow.

Things that once were a source of delight can assume a different face when they appear in the realm of self-knowledge. We can long for solitude, no doubt, when we have already found self-knowledge. But in certain moments of self-development it is solitude we have lost when we look for it as we did earlier, in moments when we flow out into the objective world, when in loneliness we have to suffer the sharpest pain.

Learning to perceive in the right way this outpouring of the Self into other beings will help us feel what has been put into the Mystery Drama: a certain artistic element has been created in which everything is spiritually realistic. One who thinks realistically—a genuine, artistic, sensitive realist—undergoes at unrealistic performances a certain amount of suffering. Even what at a certain level can provide great satisfaction is at another level a source of pain. This is due to the path of self-development. A play by Shakespeare, for instance, an immense achievement in the physical world, can be an occasion for artistic pleasure. But a certain moment of development can arrive when we are no longer satisfied by Shakespeare because we seem inwardly torn to pieces. We go from one scene to the next but no longer see the necessity that has ordered one scene to follow another. We begin to find it unnatural that a scene follows the one preceding it. Why unnatural? Because nothing holds two scenes together except the dramatist Shakespeare and his audience. His scenes follow the abstract principle of cause and effect but not a concrete reality. It is characteristic of Shakespeare's drama that nothing of underlying karma is hinted at; this would tie the scenes together more closely.

The Rosicrucian drama grew into a realistic, spiri-

23

tually realistic one. It makes huge demands on Johannes Thomasius, who is constantly on stage without taking part actively or showing a single important dramatic characteristic. He is the one in whose soul everything takes place, and what is described is the development of that soul, the real experience of the soul's development.

Johannes' soul spins one scene realistically out of the one before it. Through this we see that *realistic* and *spiritual* do not contradict each other. *Materialistic* and *spiritual* things do not need each other, and they can contradict each other. But *realistic* and *spiritual* are not opposites; it is quite possible for spiritual realism to be admired even by a materialistic person. In regard to artistic principles, the plays of Shakespeare can be thought of as realistic. You will understand, however, how far the art that goes hand in hand with a science of the spirit must finally lead. For the one who finds his Self out in the cosmos, the whole cosmos becomes an ego being. We cannot bear then anything coming toward us that is *not* related to the ego being. Art will gradually learn something in this direction; it will come to the ego principle, because the Christ has brought us our ego for the first time. In the most various realms will this ego be alive.

In still another way can the specific human entity be shown within the soul and also divided into its various components outside. If someone asked which person represents Atma, which one Buddhi, which one Manas? . . . if someone in the audience could exclaim, "O yes, that figure on the stage is the personification of Manas!" . . . it would be a horrible kind of art, a dreadful kind of art. It is a bad theosophical habit to try to explain everything like this. One would like to say, "Poor thing!" of a work of art that has to be "explained." If it were to be attempted with Shakespeare's plays, it would indeed be absurd and downright wrong.

These habits are the childhood diseases of the theo-

24

sophical movement. They will gradually be cured. But for once at least, it is necessary to point them out. It might even happen that someone tries to look for the nine members of the human organization in the Ninth Symphony of Beethoven!

On the other hand, it is correct to some extent to say that the united elements of human nature can be assigned to different characters. One person has this soul coloring, a second person another; we can see characters on the stage who present different sides of the whole unified human being. The people we encounter in the world usually present one or another particular trait. As we develop from incarnation to incarnation, we gradually become a whole. To show this underlying fact on the stage, our whole life has somehow to be separated into parts.

In this Rosicrucian Mystery we will find that everything that Maria is supposed to be is dispersed among the other figures who are around her as companions. They form with her what might be called an "egoity." We find special characteristics of the sentient soul in Philia, of the intellectual soul in Astrid, of the consciousness soul in Luna. It was for this reason that their names were chosen. The names of all the characters and beings were given according to their natures. In Devachan, Scene Seven, particularly, where everything is spirit, not only the words but also the placing of the words is meant to characterize the three figures of Philia, Astrid, and Luna in their exact relationships. The speeches at the beginning of Scene Seven are a better description of sentient soul, intellectual soul, and consciousness soul than any number of words otherwise could achieve. Here one can really demonstrate what each soul is. One can show in an artistic form the relationship of the three souls by means of the levels at which the figures stand. In the human being they flow into one another. Separated from each other, they show themselves clearly: Philia as she places herself in the cosmos; Astrid as she relates herself to the elements; Luna as she directs herself into free deed and self-knowledge. Because they show themselves so clearly in the Devachan scene, everything in it is alchemy in the purest sense of the word; all of alchemy is there, if one can gradually discover it.

Not only as abstract content is alchemy in the scene but in the weaving essence of the words. Therefore, you should listen not merely to what is said, nor indeed only to what each single character speaks, but particularly to how the soul forces speak in relation to one another. The sentient soul pushes itself into the astral body; we can perceive weaving astrality there. The intellectual soul slips itself into the etheric body; there we perceive weaving ether being. We can observe how the consciousness soul pours itself with inner firmness into the physical body. Soul endeavor that has an effect like light is contained in Philia's words. In Astrid is contained what brings about the etheric-objective ability to confront the very truth of things. Inner resolve connected at first with the firmness of the physical body is given in Luna. We must begin to be sensitive to all this. Let us listen to the soul forces in Scene Seven:

Philia *(Sentient* *soul)*	I will imbue myself with clearest essence of the light from worldwide spaces. I will breathe in sound-substance, life-bestowing, from far ethereal regions, that you, beloved sister, with your work may reach your goal.
Astrid *(Intellectual* *soul)*	And I will weave into the radiant light the clouding darkness.

26

                    I will condense
                    the life of sound,
                    that glistening it may ring
                    and ringing it may glisten,
                    that you, beloved sister,
                    may guide the rays of soul.

Luna   I will enwarm soul-substance
(Consciousness   and will make firm life-ether.
soul)   They shall condense themselves,
                    they shall perceive themselves,
                    and in themselves residing
                    guard their creative forces,
                    that you, beloved sister,
                    within the seeking soul
                    may quicken certainty of knowledge.

I would like to draw your attention to the words of
Philia,

> *Dass dir, geliebte Schwester,*
> *Das Werk gelingen kann.*

> *(that you, beloved sister, with your work*
> *may reach your goal.)*

and to those of Astrid that carry the connotation of something heavier, more compact,

> *Dass du, geliebte Schwester . . .*

"*Dass dir,*" "*Dass du,*" and then we have the "*Du*" again
in Luna's speech woven together with the still heavier,
weighty

> *Der suchenden Menschenseele*

> *(within the seeking soul)*

There the "u" is woven into its neighboring consonants,
so that it can take on a still firmer compactness.[1]

27

These are the things that one can actually characterize. Please remember, it all depends on the "How." Let
us compare the words Philia speaks next:

I will entreat the spirits of the worlds
that they, with light of being,
enchant soul feeling,
that they, with tone of words,
charm spirit hearing,

with the rather different ones of Astrid:

I will guide streams of love
that fill the world with warmth,
into the heart
of him, the consecrated one.

Just here, where these words are spoken, the inner weaving essence of the world of Devachan has been achieved.

I am mentioning all this, because the scenes should
make it clear that when self-knowledge begins to unfold
into the outer cosmic weaving and being, we have to give
up everything that is one-sided. We have to learn, too, to
be aware—as we otherwise do only in a quite superficial,
pedestrian way—of what is at hand at every point of existence. We become inflexible creatures, we human beings,
when we stay rooted to only *one* spot in space, believing
that our words can express the truth. But words, limited
as they are to physical sound, are not what best will com-
municate truth. I would like to put it like this: we have to
become sensitive to the voice itself. Anything as important as Johannes Thomasius' path to self-knowledge can
be rightfully experienced—it depends on this—only when
he struggles courageously for that self-knowledge and
holds on to it.

When self-knowledge has crushed us, the next stage is
to begin to draw into ourselves, to harbor inwardly what
was our outer experience, learning how closely the

cosmos is related to ourselves (for this comes to us after we understand the nature of the beings around us); now we must attempt courageously to live with our understanding. It is only one half of the matter to dive down like Johannes into a being to whom we have brought sorrow and have thrust into cold earth. For now we have begun to feel differently. We summon up our courage to make amends for the pain we have caused. Now we can dive into this new life and speak out of our own nature differently. This is what confronts us in Scene Nine. In Scene Two the young girl cried out to Johannes:

He brought me bitter sorrow;
I gave him all my trust.
He left me in my grief alone.
He robbed me of the warmth of life
and thrust me deep into cold earth.

In Scene Nine, however, after Johannes has undergone what every path to self-knowledge demands, the same being calls to him:

O you must find me once again
and ease my suffering.

This is the other side of the coin: first the devastation and despair, and now the return to equilibrium. The being calls to him:

O you must find me once again . . .

It could not have been described otherwise, this lifting into perception of the world, this replenishing of himself with life experience. True self-knowledge through perception of the cosmos could only have been described with the words Johannes uses when he comes to himself. It has begun, of course, in Scene Two:

For many years these words
of weighty meaning I have heard.

Then—after he has dived down into deep earth, after he has united himself with it—the power is born in his soul to let the words arise that express the essence of Scene Nine:

> *For three years now I've sought*
> *for power of soul, with wings of courage,*
> *to give these words their truth.*
> *Through them a man who frees himself can conquer*
> *and, conquering himself, can find his freedom.*

The words, "O man, unfold your being!" are in direct contrast to the words of Scene Two, "O man, know thou thyself!" There appears to us once and again the very same scene. It leads the first time downward to:

> *The world and my own nature*
> *are living in the words:*
> *O man, know thou thyself!*

Then afterward it is the opposite; it has changed. The scene characterizes soul development.

You have also heard the devastating words:

> *Maria, are you then aware*
> *through what my soul has fought its way?*
>
> . . .
>
> *For me, man's final refuge,*
> *for me, my solitude is lost.*

But Scene Nine shows how the being of the girl attains first hope and then security. That is the turning point. It cannot be constructed haphazardly; it is actual experience. Through it we can sense how self-knowledge in a soul like Johannes Thomasius can ascend into a self-unfolding. We should perceive, too, how his experience is distributed among many single persons in whom one characteristic has been formed in each incarnation.

At the end of the drama a whole community stands

30

there in the Sun Temple, like a tableau, and the many together are a single person. The various characteristics of a human being are distributed among them all; essentially there is one person there. A pedant might like to object. "Are there not too many different members of the whole? Surely nine or twelve would be the correct number!" But reality does not always work in such a way as to be in complete agreement with theory. This way it corresponds more nearly with the truth than if we had all the single constituents of man's being marching up in military rank and file.

Let us now put ourselves into the Sun Temple. There are various persons standing in the places they belong to karmically, just as their karmas have brought them together in life. But when we think of Johannes here in the middle and think, too, that all the other characters are mirrored in his soul, each character as one of his soul qualities—what is happening there if we can accept it as reality?

Johannes Thomasius

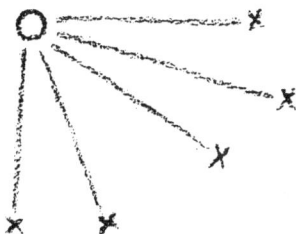

Karma has actually brought these persons together as in a focal point. Nothing is without intention, plan, or reason; what the single individualities have done not only has meaning for each one himself, but each is also a soul experience for Johannes Thomasius. Everything is hap-

31

pening twice: once in the macrocosm, a second time in the microcosm, in the soul of Johannes. This is his initiation. Just as Maria, for example, has a special connection with him, so, too, there is an important part of his soul with a similar connection to another part of his soul. Those are absolute correspondences, embodied in the drama uncompromisingly. What one sees as outer stage-happening is, in Johannes, an inner happening in his development. There has to come about what the Hierophant has described in Scene Three:

> *There forms itself within this circle*
> *a knot out of the threads*
> *which karma spins in world becoming.*

It has already formed itself, and this truly entangled knot shows what everything is leading toward. There is absolute reality as to how karma spins its threads; it is not an aimless spinning. We experience the knot as the initiation event in Johannes' soul, and the whole scene shows us a certain individuality actually standing above the others, that is, the Hierophant, who is directing, who is guiding the threads. We need only think of the Hierophant's relationship to Maria.

But it is just there that we can realize how self-knowledge can illuminate what happens to Maria in Scene Three. It is not at all pleasant, this emerging out of the Self. It is a thoroughly real experience, a forsaking of the human sheaths by our inner power; the sheaths left behind become then a battleground for inferior powers. When Maria sends down a ray of love to the Hierophant, it can only be portrayed in this way: down below, the physical body, taken over by the power of the adversary, speaks out the antithesis of what is happening above. From above a ray of love streams down, and below arises a curse. Those are the contrasting scenes: Scene Seven in

Devachan, where Maria describes what she has actually brought about, and Scene Three, where, from the deserted body, the curses of the demonic forces are directed toward the Hierophant. Those are the two corresponding scenes. They complete each other. If they had had to be "constructed" theoretically from the beginning, the end result would have been incredibly poor.

I therefore have based today's lecture on one aspect of this Mystery Drama, and I should like to extend this to include certain special characteristics that underlie initiation.

Although it has been necessary to bring out rather sharply what has just been shown as the actual events of initiation, it should not let you lose courage or resolve in your own striving toward the spiritual world. The description of dangers was aimed at strengthening a person against powerful forces. The dangers are there; pain and sorrow are the prospect. It would be a poor sort of effort if we proposed to rise into higher worlds in the most convenient way. Striving to reach the spiritual worlds cannot yet be as convenient as rolling over the miles in a modern train, one of those many conveniences our materialistic culture has put into our everyday lives. What has been described should not make us timid; to a certain extent the very encounter with the dangers of initiation should steel our courage.

Johannes Thomasius' disposition made him unable to continue painting; this grew into pain, and the pain grew into perception. So it is that everything that arouses pain and sorrow will transform itself into perception. But we have to search earnestly for this path, and our search will be possible only when we realize that the truths of spiritual science are not at all simple. They are such profound truths for our whole life that no one will ever understand them perfectly. It is just the single example in actual life that helps us to understand the world. One can speak about the conditions of a spiritual development much more exactly when one describes the development of Johannes, rather than when one describes the development of human beings in general. In the book, *Knowledge of the Higher Worlds and Its Attainment*,[2] the development that every human being can undertake is described, simply the concrete possibility as such. When we portray Johannes Thomasius, we look at a single individuality. But therewith we lose the opportunity of describing such development in a general way.

I hope you will be induced to say that I have not yet spoken out the essential truth of the matter. For we have described two extremes and must find the various gradations between them. I can give only a few suggestive ideas, which should then begin to live in your hearts and souls.

When I gave you some indications about the Gospel of St. Matthew,[3] I asked you not to try to remember the very words but to try—when you go out into life—to look into your heart and soul to discover what the words have *become*. Read not only the printed lectures, but read also in a truly earnest way your own soul.

For this to happen, however, something must have been given from outside, something has first to enter into us; otherwise, there could be self-deception of the soul. If you can begin to read in your soul, you will notice that what comes to you from outside re-echoes quite differently within. A true anthroposophical effort would be first of all to understand what is said in as many different ways as there are listeners.

No one speaking about spiritual science could wish to be understood in only one sense. He would like to be understood in as many ways as there are souls present to understand him. Anthroposophy can tolerate this. One thing is needed, however, and this is not an incidental remark; one thing is needed: every single kind of understanding should be correct and true. Each one may be individual, but it must be true. Sometimes it seems that the uniqueness of the interpretation lies in being just the opposite of what has been said.

When then we speak of self-knowledge, we should realize how much more useful it is to come to it by looking for mistakes within ourselves and for the truth outside.

It shall not be said, "Search within yourself for the truth!" Indeed, truth is to be found outside ourselves. We will find it poured out over the world. Through self-knowledge we must become free of ourselves and undergo those various gradations of soul experience. Loneliness can become a horrid companion.

We can also perceive our terrible weakness when we sense with our feelings the greatness of the cosmos out of which we have been born. But then through this we take courage. And we can make ourselves courageous enough to experience what we perceive.

Then we will finally discover that, after the loss of all the certainty we had in life, there will blossom for us the first and last certainty of life, the confidence that finding ourselves in the cosmos allows us to conquer and find ourselves anew.

O man, experience the world within yourself!
For then—in striding forth beyond your self—
You will find yourself at last
Within you own true Self.

Let us feel these words as genuine experience. They will gradually become for us steps in our development.

II

On the Rosicrucian Mystery,
The Portal of Initiation

The light of the sun is flooding
The realms of space;
The song of birds resounds
Through fields of air;
The tender plants spring forth
From Mother Earth,
And human souls rise up
With grateful hearts
To all the spirits of the world.

Those of you who were present at the performance in
Munich will remember that this children's song was the
prelude to the Rosicrucian Mystery. Tonight something
of a spiritual scientific nature should unfold itself to us in
connection with the content of this drama and with
what, one could say, has come to life in it.

If I may, I would like to touch on the long, slow spiritual path that led to this Mystery Drama. When I think
about it and look at it, its origins go back to the year 1889,
twenty-one years ago; it is not approximately but exactly
twenty-one years that bring me back to the germinal
point of this drama. In these matters absolute exactness
can be observed. The direction has been quite clear to me

in which, in 3 × 7 years, these seeds have grown (without any special assistance, I can say, on my part), for they have led their own individual life in these 3 × 7 years. It is truly remarkable to follow the path of such seeds to what may be called their finished form. Their progress can be described as a passage through the Underworld. It takes seven years for them to descend; then they return, and for this they need seven more years.

By then, having reached more or less the place where they first engaged a person before their descent, they must go in the opposite direction for seven years toward the other side; one could even say, onto a higher level. After twice seven years, then, plus seven more years, it is possible to try to embody them, foreseeing that whatever has been right in their development can take on a distinct form. If I were not convinced that within the Rosicrucian Mystery an individual organism has lived and grown for 3 × 7 years, I would not venture to speak further about it. I feel not only justified in speaking, however, though this is not really the question, but also in a sense obligated to speak about what lives in this Rosicrucian Mystery, not only between the lines, between the characters, in the What and the How, but what is alive in everything in the drama and what *must* be alive in it.

In various places since the performance of the drama in Munich, I have stated the fact that many, many things of an esoteric nature would not need to be described, that lectures would be unnecessary on my part, if only everything that lies in the Rosicrucian Mystery could work directly on your souls, my dear friends, and on the souls of others, too. I would have to use the enormous number of words necessary in my lectures and speak for days, for weeks, even for years, in order to describe what has been said and what could be said in the single drama. Everything you find in my book, *Knowledge of the Higher Worlds and Its Attainment*,[2] which is written in a somewhat tentative style—and in esoteric matters it is certainly correct to write thus as a description of the path into higher worlds—combined with what was said in *Occult Science*,[4] can be found, after all, in a much more forceful, true-to-life, and substantial form in the Rosicrucian Mystery. The reason is that it is more highly individualized. What is said in such a book as *Knowledge of the Higher Worlds* about human development had to be applicable to every individual who wishes to direct his path in some way into higher worlds, applicable to each and every person. Because of this, the book takes on—even with as much concreteness as possible—a certain abstract character, or you might call it a semi-theoretical character. We must hold fast, however, to this point: human development is never merely development in general. There is no such thing as development *per se*, no such thing as common, ordinary, orthodox development. There is only the development of this or that particular person, of a third, fourth, or twentieth human being. For each individual in the world, there must be a different process of development.

For this reason, the most honest description of the esoteric path of knowledge must have such a general character that it never in any way will coincide with an individual development. Should one actually describe the path of development as seen in the spiritual world, one can do it only by shaping the development of a single human being, by altering for the individual whatever is universally true. The book, *Knowledge of the Higher Worlds*, contains, to a certain extent, the beginning of the secrets of all human development. The Rosicrucian Mystery contains the secrets of the development of a single individual, Johannes Thomasius.

It was a truly long descent from all the occult laws of development down to a single, actually real human being. In this process, on this path, what has a tendency to become theory in *Knowledge of the Higher Worlds* had to be turned almost completely upside down. If it was to go beyond mere theory and particularly if it was to enter the artistic sphere, it had to be completely reversed, because the laws of art are quite different from any others. Just as there are natural laws, so there are also artistic laws, and these cannot be manipulated by the ordinary human consciousness, for then only dry-as-dust allegories would be the result.

Artistic laws must be handled just as Mother Nature handles her own laws when she lets a child, a plant, or an animal come into existence. If everything we can know about the world of nature is to be seen from the one direction that reveals its laws and secrets to the beholder, then whatever is to be revealed in art—any kind of art—must be seen from the other side, from just the opposite point of view. Therefore, it would be the worst imaginable interpretation of a work of art to start from ideas, concepts, or laws we have picked up somewhere, when we approach, say, a poem. Whoever thinks of explaining a work of art by means of abstract or symbolic ideas cannot be considered artistic. The poorest method of looking at a piece of work from the past in which true esoteric power has been invested, for instance, Goethe's *Faust*, would be to search within this work of art for the ideas and concepts one already has. Bad habits of this kind once prevailed in the theosophical movement in the most horrible way. I can remember something that happened just last year when we were performing Schuré's play, *The Children of Lucifer*. How shocking it was to the dramatist, who is an artist in the best sense of the word, when someone came up to him to ask, "Does this character represent Atma, this one Buddhi, a third Manas, or maybe this one is Kama Manas?" etc., etc. This kind of allegorizing is simply impossible in a truly creative, artistic process, and it is just as impossible in an explanation or inter-

40

pretation. Therefore, it can now be said that no one should be pondering the anthroposophical meaning of Johannes Thomasius. To this question there is only one answer: as the main character in the drama, he is nothing more than Johannes Thomasius. He is nothing more than the living figure, Johannes Thomasius, in whom nothing more is portrayed than the mystery of development of one man, Johannes Thomasius.

If one speaks in too general a way about the various characters, one thing will be missing, which is hinted at in the words of the drama itself:

> *There forms itself out of this circle*
> *a knot out of the threads*
> *which karma spins in world becoming.*

There is no development evolving at any point of human history without the knotting of threads within that development, "spun by karma in world becoming." And no individual development can be described without showing what is at work in the realm of the occult, that is, in the physical environment one looks at with the forces lying behind that physical environment. Therefore, Johannes Thomasius must be placed in the human surroundings out of which his development is proceeding in the real world of physical men and women.

For this reason, the drama has to have a double introduction. The Prelude shows how the cosmic world in which the threads are knotting together for Johannes, threads that "karma spins in world becoming," how this world confronts the ordinary outside world. One can certainly ask if this must be shown, if there must be a Prelude to show how this cosmic world looks from outside. Yes, it has to be shown. Something would be lacking if it were not so presented. The world in which karma spins its knots was quite different in 5000 B.C., for instance, from the world in 300 B.C. or in 1000 A.D. or today. The

41

exoteric, ordinary, outside world is always changing, too, and its own karma is connected with the environment of a person who wishes to develop himself. Thus, the circle is drawn from outside inward. On the inside is the small circle in which Johannes Thomasius stands: the second Prelude. In the ordinary world outside there are trivial waves touching the shore; in the small circle great waves are surging high. They show their turbulence, however, only within the soul of Johannes. That is why we are introduced first to the physical plane, and it is shown to us in such a way that the threads, which karma is spinning everywhere within this physical plane, are pointed out.

When you look with occult vision at any group of people, you will find that there are strands extending from one person to another, tangled in the most astonishing way. You see human beings who apparently have little to do with each other in ordinary life, but between their souls are flung the most important, most vital connections. Everything so tangled together has gradually to be illuminated, with the focus on one particular knot. Sometimes, however, whatever is in the process of becoming must be hinted at more subtly. These delicate tones had to be sounded in Scene One, where the action is taking place on the physical plane and people with a wide variety of interests are coming together. Outwardly, they chat about this or that. As they talk, however, more or less on the surface, they are revealing karma. Everyone we first meet in Scene One on the physical plane is bound to the others by destiny. What is most fundamental is *how* they are bound by destiny. None of the connections have been simply thought out; they are all based on esoteric life. All the threads can come to life, and each thread is quite unique.

The remarkable character of these connections you can guess at when you find such figures as Felix and Felicia Balde meeting with Capesius and Strader. What they

42

say is not the important thing; it is that just these persons say it. They are living persons, not invented characters. I, for one, am well acquainted with them; by that I mean they are not thought out but fully alive. They are real. I have taken especially the figure of Professor Capesius, who has grown quite dear to my heart, directly from life. The extraordinary scene of the seeress Theodora had to be brought into this setting of our ordinary world. She, as one who sometimes looks into the future, now foresees the event that is to happen before the end of the twentieth century, the coming Christ event. It is a future event that can be explained karmically, although it would be wrong to interpret other events so precisely.

Then there is the karmic relationship existing between Felicia Balde and Professor Capesius, which we find hinted at by the peculiar effect on Capesius of Felicia's fairy tales. When, too, we see Strader deeply moved by the seeress Theodora, it suggests that karmic threads are arising in Strader's heart, connecting him to her. These are all threads that lie occultly behind the physical occurrences, and they seem to be spun by karma and directed toward one point, Johannes Thomasius. In him they come together. While so much is being spoken about on the physical plane, a light begins to radiate in Johannes' soul, a light that arouses terrible waves within him. At the same time, however, this light kindles his esoteric development; as a distinctly individual development it will cross his own karma with world karma. We see, therefore, what a strong impression the happenings around him on the physical plane are making on him and how the unconscious greatness in his soul is striving upward to higher worlds.

The journey into higher worlds, however, should not take place without a compass; there must be guidance and direction. Into the midst, then, of these many relationships comes the one who is described as the leader of the group. He is also the one who understands the cosmic relationships and discerns therefore "the knots that karma spins in world becoming"; it is Benedictus, and he becomes Johannes' guide. The karma working in Johannes Thomasius, which perhaps otherwise would have to work another thousand or even thousands of years, is kindled and set ablaze in one particular moment through a karmic relationship between Benedictus and Johannes, lightly drawn in the Meditation Room scene (Scene Three). There we find ourselves at the point where a human being, destined by karma to develop himself, begins to strive upward into higher worlds. In order not to do so blindly, he will be led by Benedictus in the right direction. These thoughts will become clearer when the following passages of Scene Three are presented.

A room for meditation.
Benedictus, Johannes, Maria, and a Child.

Maria	I'm bringing you the child.
	He needs a guiding word from you.
Benedictus	My child, from now on you shall come
	to me each evening to hear the words
	that then should dwell with you
	before you enter the soul realm of sleep.
	Will you do this?
Child	I'll do it gladly.

Benedictus This evening fill your heart,
till sleep enfolds you,
with strength from these few words:
'The heavenly powers of light are carrying me
into the spirit's house.'

44

(The Child is taken out by Maria,
who then returns.)

Maria   And now that this child's destiny
shall in future flow
within the shadow of your paternal care,
I too may ask your guiding counsel,
for I've become his mother
through powers of destiny,
if not by blood.
You showed me how
to bring him up
from that first day
when I discovered him,
left by his unknown mother at my door.
And all your rules
I followed for his guidance
worked wonders on my foster child.
For every force could come to light
that in his body and his soul lay hidden.
It soon was clear that your advice
sprang from the realm
which sheltered this child's soul
before it built its body's sheath.
We saw it hopefully unfold
and shine more brightly each new day.
You know how hard it was for me at first
to gain the child's affection.
He grew up in my care,
yet nothing more than habit
first joined his soul with mine.
He looked at me, perceiving only
that I gave him all he needed
for the well-being of his body and his soul.
Then came the time when in his heart

45

love was enkindled
for me, the foster mother.
An outer cause brought forth this change.
The seeress came into our circle.
The child became attached to her
and learned, enchanted by the way she spoke,
one or the other charming word.
Then came a moment when exaltation
laid hold of our strange friend;
our child could see
the glimmering light within her eyes.
He felt his young soul shaken to the core
and, frightened, rushed to me.
From this time on
the child has been devoted
to me in warmest love.
Yet since he now received his care from me
not just through natural impulse
but with awakened feeling—
since his young heart stirs warmly
whenever he looks lovingly at me—
the treasures of your wisdom
have lost their fruitfulness.
And withered now is much
that had already ripened in the child.
I saw revealed within his being
what for my friend has proved so terrible.
I'm ever more a dark enigma to myself.
Do not deny my asking this grave question:
why do I ruin friend and child
when lovingly I try to do for them
the work that spirit guidance
lets me perceive within my heart as good?
You've shown to me the lofty truth:
illusion's veil is covering the surface of our
        life.

Yet I must have clear knowledge,
if I must bear this destiny
which is so cruel and which works such evil.

Benedictus There forms itself within this circle
a knot out of the threads
which karma spins in world becoming.
O friend, your sorrows
are part of such a knot of destiny in which
the deeds of gods entwine themselves with
      human life.
When on the pilgrimage of soul
I had attained that stage
which granted me the honor
of serving with my counsel in the spirit
      spheres,
there came to me a higher being
which should descend into the realm of earth
to take up its abode within a human body.
Man's destiny is now demanding this
at such a turning point of time.
A great step forward in our evolution
is only possible when gods
unite themselves with man's own lot.
For spirit eyes, which should awake
in human souls, can only be evolved
when first a god has laid the seed
within a human being.
The task was now assigned to me
to find that human being
who might be worthy to accept within his
      soul
the seed-force of the god.
I had to link a deed of heaven
unto a human destiny.

My spirit's eye made search—
it fell on you.
Your course of life had fitted you
as mediator for new healing forces.
In many lives you had acquired
an openness for the nobility
alive in human hearts.
The precious quality of beauty,
the highest claim of virtue,
you carried in your gentle soul
as spirit heritage.
What your eternal ego
brought down into this life through birth
matured to ripened fruit
in your first youthful years.
You did not scale too soon
the lofty spirit heights.
The longing for the spiritual world
did not arise in you
till you had fully grasped
the senses' innocent delights.
Your soul encountered love and anger while
        as yet
your thought was far away
from all desire for spirit.
To drink the joy of Nature in her beauty
and pick the fruits of art
was all you wished to find as riches in your
        life.
And you could gaily laugh
as only a small child can laugh
who has as yet no knowledge
of life's grey shadow side.
You learned to fathom human happiness,
and mourn men's pain, in times
when not an inkling had yet dawned

of questioning the roots of joy and sorrow.
The soul who shows such character
encounters earthly life
as the ripe fruit sprung from many lives.
Its childlike nature is its blossom, not
its root of being.
It was this soul alone that I could choose
as mediator for that spirit
who should attain to active power
within our human world.
So comprehend now that your being
must change into its opposite
when pouring forth from you to other beings.
The spirit in you works
in everything that can grow ripe in man
as fruit for realms eternal.
And therefore much it must destroy
that only has its place within the realm of
    time.
Its sacrifice in death, however,
is seed of immortality.
What flourishes for higher life
must bloom from death of lower being.

Maria	So this is how it stands with me. You give me light, but light that robs me of the power of sight and tears me from myself. Am I then nothing but a spirit's mediator and not my own true being? No more will I endure this form of mine, which is a mask and not the truth.
Johannes	Dear friend, what is it? Your gaze has lost its light.

Your body's turned into a pillar.
I take your hand—
and it is cold as death.

Benedictus My son, you've had to meet with many trials;
but now you stand before the hardest one.
You see her body's covering.
And yet before my gaze
her *Self* soars into spirit spheres.

Johannes O see, her lips begin to move.
She speaks . . .

Maria You gave me clarity,
yes, clarity that shrouded me
in darkness on all sides.
I curse your clarity,
and you I curse
who made of me
a tool of those wild arts
through which you seek to misguide men.
Not for one moment have I ever doubted
how high you stand in spirit.
Yet now one single instant has sufficed
to tear all faith in you out of my heart.
And I must recognize that they are hell-born
        beings,
the spirits whom you serve.
I had to mislead others
because you misled me!
I'll flee from you to regions
wherein no word of yours can penetrate,
and yet be near enough
so that my curses can still reach you!
The fire of my blood
you've torn away from me

and given to your own false god
what must be mine.
The fire of this blood,
O may it burn you!
I had to trust
in lying and deceit,
and to accomplish this
you had at first to make of me
a phantom form.
I've often had to see
how deeds and thoughts of mine
were changed into their opposite.
So now let all
that once was love for you
be changed into wild hatred's fire.
I'll hunt through all the worlds
to find that fire
that can consume you.
I cur . . . ah . . .

Johannes Who is it that is speaking here?
I do not see my friend—
I see a gruesome being!

Benedictus Maria's soul is hovering in the heights;
she's left behind her here with us
her mortal semblance only.
And where a human body
is left without a spirit,
there's room which then
the enemy of good seeks out
to step into the realm of visibility.
He finds a body's covering
and through it he can speak.
Just such an adversary spoke
who strives now to destroy the work

51

I must fulfill
for many human beings' future,
for you as well, my son.
For could I take these curses,
just spoken by Maria's vacant shell,
as other than the tempter's guile,
you should not follow me.
The enemy of good was at my side;
and you, my son, have seen
plunge down into the darkness
the temporal part of her
to whom your whole love radiates.
Because so often spirits
have spoken to you through her lips,
world karma has not spared you
from hearing through them also
the prince of hell.
Now you can seek her finally
and learn to know her being's core.
For she shall be the image of that higher man
to whom you shall aspire to raise yourself.
Her soul is soaring forth to spirit heights
where men can find their being's primal form
that in itself is rooted.
You now shall follow her to spirit realms
and see her in the Temple of the Sun.
There forms itself
within this circle
a knot out of the threads
which karma spins in world becoming.
My son, you have stood firm so far;
you will progress still further.
I see your star in its full radiance.
There is no place in sense existence
for battles such as men must fight
who strive for consecration.

What sense existence hides as riddles
which can be solved by intellect,
what human hearts receive from such
     existence—
no matter if it comes from love or hate
or whether it bursts forth with frightful
     power—
this for the spirit seeker must become
a field on which he, uninvolved,
directs his vision from without.
For forces must unfold themselves for him
which are not found upon this field itself.
You had to wrest your way through trials of
     soul
which only come to those
well armed to meet those powers
belonging to the spirit worlds.
And had those powers not found you ready
to tread the path of knowledge,
they would have had to lame your feeling
before you were allowed to know
what now has been revealed to you.
The beings who can gaze at world-
     foundations
lead men who strive into the heights
at first up to that summit
where can be shown
if they have strength
for conscious spirit sight.
Those who possess such forces
can be released out of the world of sense.
The others still must wait.
You have sustained your Self, my son,
when powers of the heights have shaken you
and spirit forces shrouded you in dread.
Your Self has strongly battled its way through,

when doubts were wrestling in your breast
and sought to give you over to dark depths.
You have been my true pupil only
since that portentous hour
when you, despairing, felt
that you yourself were lost,
and yet the strength in you still held you
    firm.
I was allowed to grant from wisdom's
    treasures
what gave you strength
to hold yourself,
though you believed no longer in yourself.
So was the wisdom which you conquered
more truthful than the faith
bestowed on you.
You are now found mature.
You now may be released.
Your friend has led the way.
In spirit you will find her.
I can still further give you the direction:
Call forth the fiery power of your soul
with words which, uttered through my
    mouth,
give you the key to spirit heights.
They will accompany you
when nothing longer guides you
which eyes of sense can still behold.
With your whole heart now willingly receive
    them:
Light's weaving essence radiates
through far-flung spaces
to fill the world with life.
Love's blessing pours its warmth
through time's long ages
to call forth revelation of all worlds.

And messengers of spirit join
light's weaving essence
with revelation of the soul.
And when with both, the human being
can join his own true self,
he is alive in spirit heights.
O spirits who can be perceived by man,
quicken with life the soul of this our son.
Let shine in him
what can illumine
his soul with spirit light.
Let sound in him
what can awaken
his self to joyous spirit growth.

Spirit Voice (behind the scene):

Thoughts now guide him
to depths of world-beginnings;
what as shadows he has thought,
what as phantoms he has felt
soars out, beyond the world of forms—
world, of whose fullness
men, when thinking,
dream in shadows;
world, from whose fullness
men, when seeing,
live within phantoms.
(As the curtain falls slowly, the music begins.)

Those last tones of music, composed by our dear
friend, Arenson,[5] bring to expression what is echoing
from higher worlds into Johannes Thomasius' soul in the
drama. It follows the solemn experience he has had in the
Meditation Room, which proved him genuinely mature

55

and strong enough to ascend into these higher worlds. At the end of the scene just recited, we hear words actually sounding out of the spiritual worlds in a completely real way, into a soul that up to a certain level, if I may so describe it, has stood the test. The imponderable had to be touched on gently with words that are more meaningful than one at first believes.

It must be quite clear that the knot spun out of the threads of world karma presents to Johannes Thomasius a fact of the most sublime and powerful nature in that solemn place. What is actually happening?

Johannes Thomasius has to perceive a soul to whom he is joined karmically in a wonderful way (as shown later in Devachan, Scene Seven), ascending directly before him into the spiritual world. It is a unique moment in world history when such a soul enters divine worlds. Naturally, not everything connected with this moment can be fully described, but it is definitely a real happening that anyone conversant with occult life will recognize in its frightening and powerful interweaving of light and shadow.

Such a person knows, too, what happens in the physical world at the shattering moment when a soul disappears into the spiritual world, not with the gradual step of individual karma but suddenly, challenged by world karma. These are moments that are vital for the evolution of mankind. They are also moments when the real, ever-present forces of temptation, peering into our physical world out of the spiritual world (just as the powers of good do), have the strength to take possession of deserted physical sheaths and use them as platforms for their guile and powers of deception. The body is the point from which they launch their attack. Immediately, then, the situation will show itself as maya, illusion, of the worst kind.

Confronted with the small deceptions of karma, a

person who is not far developed will be unable to with-stand temptation. Confronted with much greater decep-tions of karma, something that at a certain stage of devel-opment one would no longer have believed to be possible, a soul will recoil terrified, unless it has already gone through certain tragic depths of life experience. One can imagine some people saying that they, too, could have withstood what happened in the Meditation Room—but they should really find themselves sometime in the same situation! The reality is far different from what we might think it to be. In a spiritual reality strange forces are at work. If someone does not believe this, he should just consider whether or not he has had any genuine experi-ence with a human physical body abandoned by its own soul. Human beings know only ensouled bodies. In this case quite different forces come into play, and it is against these forces that Johannes Thomasius has to stand firm, having been guided to this moment in world karma.

Now two things come into question. Johannes Tho-masius first has to endure what is usually known as kamaloka, the world in which there appears to us as a mirror image what we ourselves truly are. Again, this sounds milder when spoken about than it is in reality. When it appears in its reality, there is not merely a pic-ture limited in space to tell us what it is, but it intones this from every corner of the world around us. The whole world is *we ourselves.* For this reason, when you hear in Scene Two how Johannes Thomasius descends into the depths of his soul where he is "among rocks and springs," it is not a single mirror image he conjures up, speaking to him out of his soul, but it sounds to him from everywhere around him, out of the rocks and springs, out of his whole surroundings. At such a moment, words that were tame enough as they came out of world theories or philosophi-cal works, or even spiritual scientific writings, suddenly grow into terrifying power, for they sound forth out of the whole world from every side as though, reflected from unending space, they are caught up in the various processes of nature.

O man, know thou thyself!

Thus they sound when they become audible after living year after year within the soul. The soul then is left, lonely and forsaken, and stands before its Self. Nothing is there but the world—but this world is one's own soul; it contains everything the soul is, what its karma is, everything it has perpetrated.

In a poetic work, only a special theme can be singled out—for instance, an action far in the past, the desertion of a woman—but this comes fully alive to confront Johannes Thomasius' soul. I can say only a few words about this. When it happens, Johannes loses what is necessary for him to lose: confidence in himself, in his strength, even in the ability to find in loneliness the healing for what brings him such agonizing pain on the physical plane when experiencing it there. The following words, therefore, I beg you to take as they should be taken, that is, as shaking the soul and filling it completely. When Johannes Thomasius hears from all the world around him the words, "O man, know thou thyself," his soul answers, as though his ego were not present:

For many years these words
of weighty meaning I have heard.
They sound to me from air and water;
they echo up from depths of earth.
And just as in the acorn secretly
the structure of the mighty oak is pressed,
within the power of these words
there is contained
all that my thought can comprehend
about the nature of the elements,
of souls as well as spirits,

of time and of eternity.
The world and my own nature
are living in the words:
O man, know thou thyself!

This is answered powerfully "from the springs and rocks." Then his whole inner being is turned outward:

And now! within me
it is becoming terribly alive.
Around me darkness weaves,
within me blackness yawns;
out of the world of darkness it resounds,
out of soul-blackness it rings forth:
O man, know thou thyself!

(There sounds from springs and rocks:
O man, know thou thyself!)

You must try to imagine how the Self joins the cosmic process outside. Usually, we stand still or go about our hourly tasks and fail to see what is happening out there. We have no idea of it and believe that we are within our own inner being. But Johannes is following consciously what is going on. Consciously, he keeps pace with the power of all the elements, moves with the hours of the day and transforms himself into the night.

The earth I follow in her cosmic course.
I rumble in the thunder,
I flash within the lightning.

All this leaves the impression with him: *I am.* This is the moment, however, when the *I am* becomes the Daimon of his own soul. In the process, man's self-assertion is completely silenced. One can scarcely try to speak out, "I am," but the soul replies:

. . . But oh, I feel
already separated from my being.

Then Johannes' own being appears in a limited, constrained form:

I see my body's shell.
It is an alien being outside myself;
it is remote from me.
There hovers nearer now another body . . .

Now he can no longer speak with his own mouth but with the mouth of another person. It is the woman to whom he has done a wrong:

'He brought me bitter sorrow;
I gave him all my trust.
He left me in my grief alone.
He robbed me of the warmth of life
and thrust me deep into cold earth.'

Then he returns to his own body:

She whom I left, unhappy one,
I was now she herself,
and I must suffer her despair.
Self-knowledge lent me strength
to pour myself into another self.

At this point a path is begun that is afterward described at the close of the scene in the words showing the effect of the world and the effect of solitude. In the world everything that streams in from outside works in the most frightful way. What comes from within works in such a way that the solitude is absolutely filled with people. This is a test, a test designed for the purpose hinted at in the words recited to you earlier:

The beings who can gaze at world foundations
lead men who strive into the heights
at first up to that summit
where can be shown
if they have strength

60

for conscious spirit sight.
Those who possess such forces
can be released out of the world of sense.
The others still must wait.

At this moment Johannes Thomasius would have lost consciousness and been flung back into the sense world if he had not held his ground in Scene Two, the scene we have been discussing in which he confronts his Self. Two things then became clear: his Self, as far as it is aware, has little strength; this deprives him of self-confidence. But the eternal "I" within him, of which he as yet knows nothing, has immense strength. It buoys him up and helps him to surmount the experience in the Meditation Room when Maria's soul departs. He needs, therefore, only the words of Benedictus, the force of those words, to guide him upward.

In the lines read to you, you must sense a Mystery of Words. What this means is not merely something written down in a play. In these lines cosmic forces are actually contained, down to the very sounds. Indeed, the sounds cannot be changed. The opening of a door into the spiritual world is provided by these words; therefore, they must be heard just as they are spoken. Anything of the nature of the following lines cannot be put together in an arbitrary manner:

Des Lichtes webend Wesen, es erstrahlet
Durch Raumesweiten,
Zu füllen die Welt mit Sein.
Der Liebe Segen, er erwarmet
Die Zeitenfolgen,
Zu rufen aller Welten Offenbarung.
Und Geistesboten, sie vermählen
Des Lichtes webend Wesen
Mit Seelenoffenbarung;
Und wenn vermählen kann mit beiden
Der Mensch sein eigen Selbst,
Ist er in Geisteshöhen lebend.

61

Light's weaving essence radiates
through far-flung spaces
to fill the world with life.
Love's blessing pours its warmth
through time's long ages
to call forth revelation of all worlds.
And messengers of spirit join
light's weaving essence
with revelation of the soul.
And when with both the human being
can join his own true self,
he is alive in spirit heights.

Only after this can there sound from out the other world what is to sound into the soul. These are only hints, as has been said before.

Johannes Thomasius is then really impelled into the spiritual world. He cannot, however, rise directly into this world into which every person must go; he must first pass through the astral world. In Scene Four you have the astral world represented as Johannes Thomasius perceives it on the background of his own particular, individual past experience. It is not a universal description of this world but rather a description of what, for example, Johannes Thomasius had to experience there. The astral world is quite different from the physical. It is possible to meet a person there and see him as he was decades before, or to see a young man as he will become in future years. They are both realities. In your soul nature you are still the same today as you were as a child of three. What you see in the soul world is by no means what is shown in man's outer physical form. The physical appearance conceals at every moment what was true before and what will come as truth in the future. When we look into the astral world, it is first of all necessary to overcome the primary maya of the sense world in order to understand the illusory power of *time*. For this reason Johannes Thomasius sees in the astral world the person he has met on the physical plane, Capesius, as he once was as a youth, and he sees the one he knows as Strader just as he will be as an old man. What does this mean? Johannes knows Strader as he is now in the sense world with the forces present in his soul on the physical plane. But already within Strader are the conditions for what he will become after several decades. This also has to be included in our knowledge of a human being. Thus, time is rent asunder. It is really so that time is quite elastic in its nature when one enters the higher worlds. In the physical world Johannes Thomasius knows Capesius as elderly, Strader as young; now they stand together in the astral world: Capesius young, Strader old. It is not that time is stretched forward and backward but that one man is shown in his youth, the other in his old age. It is an absolutely real fact.

Something more is shown in this scene, something people react to with adolescent scorn. This is the fact that our soul experiences are greater than we usually think they are, that good and bad have their consequences when experienced within the soul. For example, if we think thoughts that are cruel or even false, they stream into the depths of the world and back again; we are closely connected in our soul experiences with the elemental powers of nature. This is no mere image. From the esoteric point of view, for example, it is a reality when Capesius is brought before the Spirit of the Elements, who leads every human being into existence. Actually Capesius is confronting what the Spirit of the Elements is concerned with—and concerned with in such a way that when we experience anything in the soul, it is related to the elemental forces of nature. Johannes Thomasius is shown that both Capesius and Strader, out of the depths of their souls, can arouse the opposing powers of the ele-

63

ments. In that world, therefore, thunder and lightning follow what they have felt in their souls as pride or haughtiness, error, truth or lies. In the physical world the error or lie a person has in his soul is quite peculiar. Someone can stand before us with error and lying in his soul and may appear to be quite innocent. But the moment we look at him with astral vision, we can see raging storms that otherwise are represented on earth only as a picture by the most terrible convulsions of the elements. All this Johannes has to experience and everything, too, that in the astral world can show him the remarkable connections he did not recognize when he met them on the physical plane.

The names given in this Rosicrucian Mystery are not given just by chance. Names such as "the Other Maria," and so on, all point to definite relationships, so that the "one" and the "other" Maria are not merely "two Marias" but present themselves as Maria-forces to the other characters. "The Other Maria," the mysterious nature figure, is revealed to Johannes Thomasius as the soul living below the ordinary conscious soul quite inaudibly and imperceptibly as long as man lives only in the physical world. But you must not take these relationships and characters as symbols. The Other Maria is absolutely a real person, a reality, just as the first Maria is. They should be taken for what they really are.

Everything that Johannes Thomasius has experienced passes before the eyes of his soul. He has experienced the astral world. This he can now bring into his consciousness by saying:

In realms of soul I find again
the human beings who are known to me.
The man who spoke about Felicia's fairy tales:
I could behold him here

64

as in his younger years;
and also he who as a youth
had chosen to become a monk:
here as an old man he appeared to me.
And with them was the Spirit of the Elements.

(End of Scene Four)

Johannes Thomasius has passed through what wipes out time before his eyes, because he has now become mature, sufficiently mature to see into the astral world. Is this world free from error? No, it is not. But in the astral world one thing can become a certainty for man. It will become a certainty for him, if he enters it in purity and without guilt, that there is a higher world shining into the astral world, just as the astral world shines into the ordinary physical world. The only question is whether or not he can see this as it actually is. People who go about in this physical world are themselves only a kind of illusion, in that they have something behind them leading them into the higher world. They stand in contrast to what they have perhaps been in distant or more recent times and what they will become in the future. But certain errors do not show us the astral world in which one is quite entangled in the world of the senses. For instance, they do not show the relationship of the three great forces of our existence: Will, Love, and Wisdom. This is so difficult to discern and understand in its reality that it remains hidden for a long time in the astral world. It is not an easy matter to discover it there. Besides, some relationships that are errors in the sense world are continued on into the astral world.

The working together of will, wisdom, and love, which at this point can only be touched on, takes place in the physical world through human beings. In the higher worlds it takes place through the beings who expend their

65

forces whenever, on the physical plane, the forces of supersensible beings descend into human souls. This happens through initiates in those temples where there are human representatives for the single world-forces, where human beings have come so far as to renounce the desire to portray the whole human being as he is but limit themselves to portraying a single force. It is the representatives who have taken over. But when man looks into the astral world, those holy places of the representatives of the powers of will, wisdom, and love are shown to him in a picture filled with maya. Therewith is woven a fearful web between the illusion of the sense world and of the astral world.

Now, I should have to talk for weeks if I wished to explain how it is with that figure of the higher powers shown as the initiate of the powers of will; he has met Johannes Thomasius on the physical plane, and there he really seems to be an ordinary, superficial fellow. In such a case the question can arise: are the primal forces of will supposed to work through such a person? Yes, they are. We can perhaps understand that the force manifesting the powers of will can permeate just this kind of less developed human being in the same way as the radiance of wisdom enters a man like Benedictus. We must grasp the following. If we have a beautiful flower in full bloom and place a seed beside it, it may be that the seed when developed will bring forth a still more beautiful flower. The flower can at this moment be considered quite perfect, but, according to cosmic reality, the seed is actually something more perfect. Hence, we have these opposites: Benedictus, the eminent bearer of wisdom, and the man who on the physical plane behaves in such a strange way toward everything said about the spiritual worlds and in such a strange way rejects it all. When in a group of people he hears talk about the spiritual worlds, he says, as if he were unwilling to listen:

66

I cannot find the bridge
that leads across
from mere ideas to actual deeds.

(Romanus, Scene One)

He is a man who finds elsewhere what leads to deeds; to him, any talk about the spiritual is simply empty talk. You could tell this fellow beautiful things about theosophy; to the man he is, now, on the physical plane, it is nothing but words. What he finds worthwhile is the working of machines. When he hears about the Other Maria, how spiritual power has become part of her, kindling a strength of feeling and love in her so that she can perform healing deeds, he is the one who rejects all this, saying merely, "That comes from her having a good heart!" He remains wholly on the physical plane, where he is indeed a philistine, an ordinary fellow, but also at the same time an energetic, determined man of will. Hence he says:

If this good person has achieved so much
the impulse lies
in her warm heart.
When work is done, men surely need
refreshment and renewal from ideas.
But only training of the will,
combined with skill and strength
in all the genuine work of life,
will further human progress.
When whirr of wheels
is humming in my ears,
and when contented human hands
are labouring at machines,
it's then I feel the powers of life at work.

This is the man of will, the man of action. If you were to talk to him day in and day out about the spirit, his only response would be, "You can't turn a winch with that; meanwhile, what are people going to eat?" This amounts to saying, "Turn your winches all day long, and then, if you have a little spare time, talk about the spirit for amusement!" Here are the forces still latent in the seed, and they are good forces, important forces. Through the powers of will they stream into the world. When people hear about spiritual worlds and receive what is said, each in his own way, this must not be judged theoretically, for it is extremely difficult to arrive at the truth. If you do not understand that a seed must be looked upon as the counterpart to such a person as has just been described, you will be experiencing the same kind of illusion as the one presented by the Subterranean Temple. There it is an astral maya. There is reality in what Johannes Thomasius perceives in the scene with Capesius and Strader when he sees them at different ages. But in Scene Five a maya, a Fata Morgana of the spiritual world, is pictured, from which, after it has been experienced, the soul must free itself. Therefore, you have to take Scene Five as justified only by the fact that reality is intermingled with the maya.

No part of this scene would contribute to Johannes Thomasius' development unless it bore the same relationship to astral experience that the concepts and ideas of the physical world bear to our understanding of the world. What scientific knowledge is for the physical plane, the "Maya Temple" is for the astral world. The "Maya Temple" is no more a reality rooted in the spiritual world than a concept is something we can eat. But concepts must live in the world for an understanding of the world to be possible. Only in this way can there play in from another world what is profoundly illuminating for Johannes Thomasius, that is, to recognize the definite knot in world karma formed when Felix Balde comprehends that in solitary wanderings about the world he must not bury his soul treasures but must bring them to the temple.

Then, for the first time, it is possible for Johannes Thomasius to perceive relationships in the spiritual world that are, so to speak, much more real, and of a more delicate and intimate nature. For example, the projection of the astral world into the physical world takes place when such a thing happens as the inspiring of a man like Capesius by someone who does not really know, herself, how much is living in her soul. In the Mystery Play, Felicia Balde does not know this. In the case of a man of intellect, a man who works intellectually, everything passes through his intellect. There is nothing whatever in the intellect that can give us strength while it instructs us about the world. This lies outside the capacity of the intellect. In a person of exceptional intelligence, a force coming from the spiritual world may pass through the intellect and then continue. At this point, he will be able to speak of the spiritual world in splendid, theoretical terms. The mind, however, does not influence the degree of inner esoteric life or the content of the soul. What comes from theories may reach the soul even without passing through the intellect; it can discover a person who is receptive to the fountainhead of spirit and who can summon up something there that Capesius, for instance, describes on the physical plane. This is clearly shown in his words about Felicia Balde, who lives out there in the solitude with Felix, and what she really means to him—when he says how gladly he listens to her because she speaks out of the most profound, age-old wisdom. It is important for us to grasp fully what Capesius is saying: on the physical plane there is a woman to whom he likes to listen and from whose lips come things welling up from occult sources. She cannot clothe them in elegant words, but when her words reach the ear of Capesius, he can say:

I must allude
if I'm to tell about it,
to something which in truth

seems far more wonderful to me
than much that I have heard of here,
because it speaks more to my heart.
I scarcely should be able in another place
to bring the words across my lips
which here I find so easy.
I feel my soul, at times,
as though entirely empty and exhausted;
it is as if the very fountainhead
of knowledge had run dry within me,
as if I could not find one word
that seems worthwhile to speak or to be heard.
(Scene One)

Such things exist. Such people, however much they know, feel at these times as if they could get no further.

And when I feel such barrenness of spirit,
then I escape and go where these good people
have their refreshing, quiet solitude.

Then his soul begins to open out, because that is for him the door into the occult world.

And there Felicia tells me many a tale
in pictures fabulous,
of beings dwelling in the land of dreams
and in the realm of magic fairy tales,
who live a motley life.
The tone in which she tells of them
recalls the bards of ancient times.
I do not ask the sources of her words,
but this one thing I clearly know:
that new life wells and flows into my soul
dispelling its paralysis.

The reality of all this Johannes Thomasius can observe on the physical plane, for he is present, but to be able to explain it to himself he has first to look into the astral world. In Scene Six then, in the astral world, Felicia Balde appears to him "just as she is in life." She gives the Spirit of the Elements one of the hundreds of fairy tales she has told Capesius. Now, however, comes the reciprocal movement to what takes place below the threshold of consciousness.

Felicia has told Capesius her fairy tales. When she tells one that she herself does not understand, the forces arise in his soul that banish his mental paralysis; then he can, in turn, relate something to his audience. It sounds, however, quite different from what Felicia has related. Mysterious forces are active even in Capesius. When one seeks to discover them, he will find their origin in the astral world, where it can be seen how they call forth countercurrents. Wherever there are elemental powers, they call up the kind of reverberations that Felicia's words awaken in the soul of Capesius. The same kind of thing occurs in our brain. A little spirit lives there who perhaps thinks out the most wonderful things. When we try to discover how he comes out of the macrocosm, we are likely to find the Earth-brain, which thinks thoughts on quite a different scale from those appearing in the small human brain. A man will often assert something he does not see in his own brain, but it will look grotesque when it is reflected in the giant Earth-brain. This has to be reflected; hence, the relationship of Gairman, who appears on the physical plane and then as the Spirit of the Earth-brain. About this, too, one could speak for a long time. Were we to look with soul vision at what takes place in the lonely cottage when Felicia tells her fairy tales and afterward behold the Spirit of the Earth-brain, we would discover many a secret, as, for instance, how ironical this Spirit of the Earth-brain is and how often he mocks. Ridicule has to be a concern of his, because he finds much to laugh at in what human beings do.

From an artistic point of view it is justifiable that the

moment this mockery is out of place, Gairman appears in the role he has so often to play and shows himself in his true guise. We see then, after Felicia Balde has told one of her fairy tales before the Spirit of the Elements in Scene Six, how an abnormal effect is produced on the Spirit of the Earth-brain, who translates the tale in quite different words. Felicia relates the story:

. . . Once upon a time
there was a Being
that flew from East to West,
following the journey of the sun.
It flew on, over lands and over seas;
and from the heights it watched
the busy life of men.
It saw how men love one another,
and how in hate they persecute each other.
Nothing could hinder
this Being in its flight;
for hate and love create
always the same a thousandfold.
But over one house on its way
the Being had to pause.
Within, there was a tired man
who pondered over human love
and pondered, too, on human hate.
His pondering had carved
deep furrows on his brow,
had turned his hair quite white.
In its concern for him,
the Being lost its guide, the sun,
and stayed at this man's side.
It was still in his room
at evening when the sun went down;
and when the sun returned,
the Being was once more
caught upward by the spirit of the sun.

72

Again it saw the many people
in love, in hate,
continue on their earthly course.
And when it came a second time
above the house, still following the sun,
its gaze fell there
upon a dead old man.

The Spirit of the Earth-brain responds in a way that is
naturally not at all justifiable:

Once upon a time there was a man
who tramped from East to West;
the urge for knowledge lured him on
to travel over lands and seas,
and by his rules of wisdom
he watched the busy life of men.
He saw how men love one another
and how in hate they persecute each other.
At every single instant
he saw himself at all his wisdom's end.
For how it is that hate and love
forever rule the earthly world
could not be brought into a law.
He noted many thousand cases,
yet lacked a comprehensive whole.
This dry researcher
encountered on his way
a Being of the Light,
upon whom life weighed heavily,
for it was in a constant battle
with a dark shadow-form.
'Well, who are you?'
inquired the dry researcher.
'Oh, I am Love,'
one being answered.
'In me behold dark Hate,'

so spoke the other.
The man, however, could
no longer hear these beings' words.
As deaf researcher, he tramped on
from East to West, this man.

These things are distinct experiences of the astral world. Johannes Thomasius has to pass through them in order to ascend into the spiritual world.

Today I will only say briefly that it is necessary for Johannes Thomasius, in order to reach the spiritual world itself, to make a real connection with that world on threads already woven in the physical world. As you will hear later in the recitation of Scene Seven, his connection with the spiritual world arose out of the karma encompassed by incarnations, and this could be revealed only to Devachanic vision. Devachanic elements actually have to play their part. Therefore, I ask you to notice how everything is alive in the living, weaving Devachanic ocean. This can be described, but the details must more or less be hinted at. For a real description we must go further. Let us not think that we know anything of higher worlds by speaking about them with the words sentient soul, intellectual soul, consciousness soul, alluding to Philia, Astrid, and Luna. These three figures are in no way personifications of the three soul principles, nor are they symbols for them. Listen to the vowels with which each of these characters describes her activities. Try to hear what lives in the vowels. Then you can follow how the sequence of single vowels and single words make clear what is given in a different way as sentient, intellectual, and consciousness souls. Should you delete any part of it, it will no longer be intact. Therefore, it is important to listen carefully to the words when, for instance, Luna speaks, so as to get an understanding of the Devachanic element in the consciousness soul:

74

Ich will erwärmen Seelenstoff
Und will erhärten Lebensäther.
Sie sollen sich verdichten,
Sie sollen sich erfühlen,
Und in sich selber seiend
Sich schaffend halten,
Dass du, geliebte Schwester,
Der suchenden Menschenseele
Des Wissens Sicherheit erzeugen kannst.
I will enwarm soul-substance
and will make firm life-ether.
They shall condense themselves,
they shall perceive themselves,
and in themselves residing
guard their creative forces,
that you, beloved sister,
Within the seeking soul
may quicken certainty of knowledge.
(Scene Seven)

In the movement of the words can be heard in this
description of Devachan what otherwise cannot in any
way be expressed. This, too, must be taken into consider-
ation. When speaking about higher worlds, we are definitely obliged to speak in many different ways. What I
could never say theoretically about the sentient, intellectual, and consciousness souls you may perceive, if you
have the desire to understand it, from the characterization of the three figures, Philia, Astrid, and Luna. But
you must understand that these three are not symbols or
allegories of the sentient, intellectual, and consciousness
souls. Should you ask, "What are these three?" the
answer would be, "They are persons who are alive; they
are Philia-, Astrid-, and Luna-people." This always must
be kept firmly in mind.

75

How karma, finally intertwining and twisting itself together, can display in a picture what as microcosm Johannes Thomasius experiences in his soul—this was portrayed in the whole closing scene of the Munich performance. Showing how karma is at work, the various characters stood in their places. Each had his position according to his relationship to another person. If you imagine this actually mirrored in the soul of Johannes Thomasius, you will then have more or less what is contained in this picture of the spirit realm in Scene Seven, which could only with great difficulty be given verbal expression.

(There followed a recitation of Scene Seven by Marie von Sivers, accompanied at the beginning and end by the music of Adolf Arenson.)

III

Symbolism and Phantasy in Relation to the Mystery Drama, *The Soul's Probation*

Let us consider today the second Mystery Drama, *The Soul's Probation*. You will have noticed that in our various stage performances, and especially in this play, an attempt was made to bring the dramatic happenings into connection with our anthroposophical world view. In this play in particular, we wanted to present on the stage in a very real way the idea of reincarnation and its effect on the human soul. I need not say that the incidents in *The Soul's Probation* are not simply thought out; they fully correspond with observations of esoteric study in certain ways, so that the scenes are completely realistic in a definite sense of the word. We can discuss this evening first of all the idea that a kind of transition had to be created, leading from Capesius' normal life to his plunge into a former life, into the time when he lived through his previous incarnation.

I have often asked myself since *The Soul's Probation* was written, what enabled Capesius to build a bridge from his life in a world where he had known—though certainly with a genial spirit—only what is given by external sense perception with a world view bound to the instrument of the brain; how it was, I say, that a bridge could be created from such a world to the one into which he then plunged, which could only be revealed through occult sense organs. I have often asked myself why the fairy tale, with the three figures at the rock spring (Scene Five) had to be the bridge for Capesius. Of course, it was not because of some clever idea or some deliberate decision that the fairy tale was placed just at this point, but simply because imagination brought it about. One could even ask afterward why such a fairy tale is necessary. In connection, then, with *The Soul's Probation* there came to me certain enlightening points of view about the poetry of fairy tales in general and about poetry in relation to anthroposophy.

A person could well put into practical use in his life the facts implicit in the division of the soul into sentient, intellectual, and consciousness souls, but when he does, riddles of perception will loom up in a simply elemental-emotional way with regard to his place in, and relationship to, the world. These riddles do not allow themselves to be spoken out in our ordinary language, with our ordinary concepts, for the simple reason that we are living today in too intellectual a time to bring to expression in words, or through what is possible in words, the subtle distinctions between the three members of our soul.

It is better to choose a method that will allow the soul's relationship to the world to seem diversified and yet quite definite and clear. What moves through the whole of *The Soul's Probation* as the connecting link between the events themselves and what is significant in the three figures, Philia, Astrid, and Luna, had to be expressed in delicate outlines; yet this had to call up strong enough soul responses to bring out clearly man's relationship to the world around him. It could be presented in no other way than to show how the telling of the fairy tale about the three women awoke in Capesius' soul, as a definite preparation for his development, the strong urge to descend into those worlds that only now are beginning to be perceived again by human beings as real.

78

There will now be a recital of the fairy tale, so that we can reflect upon it afterward.

*

(Scene Five: Tale of the Rockspring Wonder)

Once upon a time there was a boy
who lived—the only child of a poor forester—
within a woodland solitude. He knew
besides his parents hardly any other people.
His build was slender,
his skin almost transparent.
One could look long into his eyes:
they treasured deepest spirit wonders.
And though indeed few people entered
the circle of his life,
he never was in need of friends.
When in the nearby mountains
the golden sunlight glowed and glimmered,
the boy's rapt, musing eye drew forth
the spirit gold into his soul
until his heart resembled
the morning brightness of the sun.—
But when through darkening clouds
the morning sunrays could not pierce
and dreariness hung over mountain heights,
the boy's eye, too, grew dull;
a mood of sadness filled his heart.—
The spirit weaving of his narrow world
took hold of him so fully
that it was no less strange to him
than were his body and his limbs.
The trees and flowers of the woods
were all his friends:
there spoke to him from crown and calyx
and from the lofty tree-tops spirit beings
and what they whispered, he could understand.—

Such wondrous things of worlds unknown
unlocked themselves before the boy
whenever his soul conversed
with what most people would regard as lifeless.
At evening his anxious parents
from time to time missed their beloved child.—
The boy was at a spot nearby
where from the rocks a spring burst forth,
and waterdrops, dispersing thousandfold,
were scattered over stones.
When moonlight's silver glance,
in sparkling colours' sorcery,
was mirrored in the water's misty spray,
the boy could sit for hours on end
beside the rock-born spring.
And figures, formed by spirit-magic,
arose before his youthful vision
in rushing water and in moonlight's glimmer.
They grew into three women's forms
who told him of those things
toward which his soul's desire was turned.—
And when upon a gentle summer night
the boy was sitting at the spring again,
one woman of the three caught up a myriad of
        drops
out of the glittering spray
and gave them to the second woman.
She fashioned from the tiny drops
a chalice with a silver gleam
and passed it to the third.
She filled it with the moonlight's silver rays
and gave it to the boy,
who had beheld all this
with youthful inner sight.—
Now in the night
which followed this event,

he dreamed that he was robbed
by a fierce dragon of the chalice.
After this night the boy beheld
just three times more the wonder of the spring.
Henceforth the women came no more
although the boy sat musing
beside the rock-born spring in moonlight's silver
    sheen.
And when three hundred sixty weeks
had run their course three times,
the boy had long become a man
and left his parents' home and forest country
to live in a strange city.
One evening, tired from the day's hard toil,
he pondered on what life had still in store for him,
and suddenly he felt himself a boy,
caught up and carried to his rock-born spring.
Again he could behold the water-women
and this time heard them speak.
The first one said to him:
   Remember me at any time
   you feel alone in life.
   I lure man's eye of soul
   to starry spaces and ethereal realms.
   And whosoever wills to feel me,
   I offer him the draught of hope in life
   out of my wonder goblet. —
And then the second spoke:
   Do not forget me at the times
   when courage in your life is threatened.
   I lead man's yearning heart
   to depths of soul and up to spirit heights.
   And whosoever seeks his strength from me,
   for him I forge the steel of faith in life,
   shaped by my wonder hammer. —
The third one could be heard:

To me lift up your eye of spirit
when your life's riddles overwhelm you.
I spin the threads of thought that lead
through labyrinths of life and the abyss of soul.
And whosoever harbours trust in me,
for him I weave the living rays of love
upon my wonder loom.—
Thus it befell the man,
and in the night that followed this
he dreamed a dream:
a savage dragon prowled
in circles round about him,—
and yet could not come near him.
He was protected from that dragon by
the beings he had seen beside the rock-born spring
and who with him had left his home
for this far-distant place.

It seems to me that the world of fairy tales can quite
rightfully be placed between the external world and
everything that in past times man, with his early clairvoyance, could see in the spiritual world; with everything, too, that he can still behold today if, by chance,
either through certain abnormal propensities or through
a trained clairvoyance, he can raise himself to the
spiritual world. Between the world of spirit and the
world of outer reality, of intelligence, of the senses, it is
the world of the fairy tale that is the most fitting connecting link. It would seem necessary to find an explanation
for this position of the fairy tale and the fairy tale mood
between these other two worlds.

It is extraordinarily difficult to create the bridge be
tween these spheres, but I realized that a fairy tale itse'f
could construct it. Better than all the theoretical explana-
tions, a simple fairy tale really seems to build this bridge,
a tale that one could tell something like this:

Once upon a time there was a poor boy who owned nothing but a clever cat. The cat helped him win great riches by persuading the King that her master possessed an estate so huge, so remarkably beautiful that it would amaze even the King himself. The clever cat brought it about that the King set forth and traveled through several astonishing parts of the country. Everywhere he went, he heard—thanks to the cat's trickery—that all the great fields and strange buildings belonged to the poor boy.

Finally, the King arrived at a magnificent castle, but he came a bit late (as often happens in fairy tales), for it was just the time when the Giant Troll, who was the actual owner of this wonderful place, was returning home from his wanderings over the earth, intending to enter his castle.

The King was inside looking at all its wonders, and so the clever cat stretched herself out in front of the entrance door, for the King must not suspect that everything belonged to the Giant Troll. It was just before dawn that the Giant arrived home and the cat began to tell him a long tale, holding him there at the front door to listen to it. She rattled along about a peasant plowing his field, putting on manure, digging it in, going after the seed he wanted to use, and finally sowing the field. In short, she told him such an endless tale that dawn came and the sun began to rise. The wily cat told the Giant to turn around and look at the Golden Maid of the East whom he surely had never seen before. But when he turned to look, the Giant Troll burst into pieces, for that is what happens to giants and is a law they have to conform to: they may not look at the rising sun. Therefore, through the cat's delaying the Giant, the poor boy actually came into possession of the wonderful palace. The clever cat at first had given her master only hope, but finally, with her tricks, also the great castle and the vast estate.

One can say that this simple little tale is extremely

83

significant for its explanation of fairy tale style today. It is really so that when we look at men and women in their earthly development, we can see what most of them are —those who have developed on earth in the various incarnations they have lived through and are now incarnated. Each one is a "poor boy." Yes, in comparison to earlier historical epochs, today we are fundamentally "poor boys" who possess nothing but a clever cat. We do, however, it's true, have a clever cat, which is our intelligence, our intellect. Everything the human being has acquired through his senses, whatever he now possesses of the outer world through the intelligence limited to the brain, is absolute poverty in comparison to the whole cosmic world and to what man experienced in the ancient Saturn, Sun, and Moon epochs. All of us are basically "poor boys," possessing only our intelligence, something that can exert itself a little in order to promise us some imaginary property. In short, our modern situation is like the boy with the clever cat.

Actually, though, we are not altogether the "poor boy"; that is only in relation to our consciousness. Our ego is rooted in the secret depths of our soul life, and these secret depths are connected with endless worlds and endless cosmic happenings, all of which affect our lives and play into them. But each of us who today has become a "poor boy" knows nothing more of this splendor; we can at best, through the cat, through philosophy, explain the meaning and importance of what we see with our eyes or take in with our other senses. When a modern person wants somehow to speak about anything beyond the sense world, or if he wishes to create something that reaches beyond the sense world, he does it, and has been doing it for several hundred years, by means of art and poetry.

Our modern age, which in many ways is a peculiarly transitional one, points up strongly how men and women fail to escape the mood of being "poor boys," even when

84

they can produce poetry and art in the sense world. For in our time (1911), there is a kind of disbelief in trying to aim toward anything higher in art than naturalism, the purely external mirroring of outer reality. Who can deny that often today when we look at the glittering art and literature expressing the world of reality, we can hear a melancholy sigh, "Oh, it's only delusion; there's no truth in any of it." Such a mood is all too common in our time. The King of the fairy tale, who lives in each one of us and has his origin in the spiritual world, definitely needs to be persuaded by the clever cat—by the intelligence given to man—that everything growing out of the imagination and awakened by art is truly a genuine human possession. Man is persuaded at first by the King within him but only for a certain length of time. At some point, and today we are living just at the beginning of such a time, it is necessary for human beings to find once more the entrance to the spiritual, divine world. It is today necessary for human beings, and everywhere we can feel an urgency in them, to rise again toward the spheres of the spiritual world.

There has first, however, to be some sort of bridge, and the easiest of all transitions would be a thoughtful activating of the fairy tale mood. The mood of the fairy tale, even in a quite superficial sense, is truly the means to prepare human souls, such as they are today, for the experience of what can shine into them from higher, supersensible worlds. The simple fairy tale, approaching modestly with no pretension of copying everyday reality but leaping grandly over all its laws, provides a preparation in human souls for once more accepting the divine, spiritual worlds. A rough faith in the divine worlds was possible in earlier times because of man's more primitive constitution, which gave him a certain kind of clairvoyance. But in the face of reality today, this kind of faith has to burst into pieces just as the Giant Troll did. Only through clever cat questions and cat tales, spun about everyday reality, can we hold him back. Certainly we can spin those endless tales of the clever cat to show how here and there external reality is forced toward a spiritual explanation.

In broad philosophical terms one can spin out a long-winded answer to this or that question only by referring to the spiritual world. One still keeps all this as a kind of memento from earlier times; with it one can succeed in detaining the Giant for a short time. What is with us from earlier times, however, cannot hold its own against the clear language of reality. It will burst into pieces just as the Giant Troll burst, on looking at the rising sun. But one has to recognize this mood of the bursting Giant. It is something that has a relationship to the psychology of the fairy tale. Because I find it impossible to describe such things theoretically, I can get at this psychology only through observing the nature of the human soul. Let me say the following about it.

Think for a moment how there might appear livingly, imaginatively, before someone's soul what we recently described in the lectures about pneumatosophy,[6] depicting briefly some details of the spiritual world. In these anthroposophical circles we certainly speak a good deal about the spiritual world. Before a person's soul, it should come at first as a living imagination. There would be little explicit description, however, if you intended only to describe what urges itself forward toward the soul, even toward the clairvoyant soul. A queer sort of disharmony comes about when one mixes such truths as those about ancient Saturn, Sun, and Moon conditions, as described in our last three anthroposophical meetings,[7] into the dismal, ghostlike thoughts of modern times. Over against those things raised up before the soul, one is aware of man's narrow limits. Those secrets of divine worlds have to be grasped, it would seem, by something in us resembling a troll. A swollen, troll-like giant is what one becomes when trying to catch hold of the pictures of the spiritual world. Before the rising sun, then, one has voluntarily to let the pictures burst in a certain way in order for them to be in accord with the mood of modern times. But you can hold something back; you can hold back just what the "poor boy" held back. For our immediate, present-day soul to be left in possession of something, you need the transformation, the matter-of-fact transformation, of the gigantic content of the world of the imagination into the subtlety of the fairy tale mood. Then the human soul will truly feel like the King who has been guided to look at what the soul, this "poor boy" soul, actually does not possess. Nevertheless, it does come into possession of riches when the gigantic Troll bursts into pieces, when one sacrifices the imaginative world in the face of external reality and draws it into the palace that one's phantasy is able to erect.

In former times the phantasy of the "poor boy" was nourished by the world of the imagination, but in view of today's soul development this is no longer possible. If, however, we first of all give up the whole world of the imagination and press the whole thing into the subtle mood of the fairy tale, which does not rely on everyday reality, something can remain to us in the fairy tale phantasy that is deep, deep truth. In other words, the "poor boy," who has nothing but his cat, the clever intellect, finds in the fairy tale mood just what he needs in modern times to educate his soul to enter the spiritual world in a new way.

It therefore seems to me from this point of view to be psychologically right that Capesius, educated so completely in the modern world of ideas, though certainly with quite a spiritual regard for this world, should come to the realm of the fairy tale as something new that will open for him a genuine relationship to the occult world. So there had to be something like a fairy tale written into the scene to form a bridge for Capesius between the world of external reality and the world into which he was to plunge, beholding himself in an earlier incarnation.

What has just been described as a purely personal remark about the reason I had for putting the fairy tale at this very place in the drama coincides with what we can call the history of how fairy tales arose in mankind's development. It agrees wonderfully with the way that fairy tales appeared in human lives. Looking back into earlier epochs of human development, we will find in every prehistoric folk a certain primitive kind of clairvoyance, a capacity to look into the spiritual world. Therefore, we must not only distinguish the two alternating conditions of waking and sleeping in those early times, with a chaotic transition of dream as well, but we must assume in these ancient people a transition between waking and sleeping that was not merely a dream; on the contrary, it was the possibility of looking into reality, living with a spiritual existence. A modern man, awake, is in the world with his consciousness, but only with his sentient consciousness and with his intelligence. He has become as poor as the boy who had nothing but a clever cat. He can also be in the spiritual world in the night, but then he is asleep and is not conscious of it. Between these two conditions, early man had still a third, which conjured something like magnificent pictures before his soul. He lived then in a real world, one that a clairvoyant who has attained the art of clairvoyance also experiences as a world of reality, but not dreamlike or chaotic. Still, ancient man possessed it to such a degree that he could en-compass his imaginations with conscious clarity. He lived in these three different conditions. Then, when he felt his soul widening out into the spiritual cosmos, finding its connection with spiritual beings of another kind close to the hierarchies, close to the spiritual beings living in the elements, in earth, water, air, and fire, when he felt his whole being widening out from the narrow limits of his existence, it must have been for him, in these in-between conditions, like the Giant who nevertheless burst into pieces when the sun rose and he had to wake up.

These descriptions are not at all unrealistic. Because today one no longer feels the full weight of words, you might think the words "burst into pieces" are put there more or less carelessly, just as a word often is merely added to another. But the bursting into pieces actually describes a specific fact. There came to the ancient human being, after he had felt his soul growing out into the entire universe and then, with the coming of the Golden Maid of the Morning, had had to adapt his eyes to everyday reality, there came to him the everyday reality like a painful blow thrusting away what he had just seen. The words really describe the fact.

But within us there is a genuine King, which is a strong and effective part of our human nature; he would never let himself be prevented from carrying something into our world of ordinary reality out of that world in which the soul has its roots. What is thus carried into our everyday world is the projection or reflection of experi-ence; it is the world of phantasy, a real phantasy, not the fantastic, which simply throws together a few of the rags and tatters of life, but it is true phantasy, which lives deep in the soul and which can be urged out of there into every phase of creating. Naturalistic phantasy goes in the

89

opposite direction from genuine phantasy. Naturalistic phantasy picks up a motif here and a motif there, seeks the patterns for every kind of art from everyday reality and stitches these rags of reality together like patchwork. This is the one and only method in periods of decadent art.

With the kind of phantasy that is the reflection of true imagination, there is something at work of unspecified form, not this shape nor that, and not yet aware of what the outer forms will be that it wants to create. It feels urged on by the material itself to create from within outward. There will then appear, like a darkening of the light-process, what inclines itself in devotion to external reality as image-rich, creatively structured art. It is exactly the opposite process from the one so often observed in today's art work. From an inner center outward everything moves toward this true phantasy, which stands behind our sense reality as a spiritual fact, an imaginative fact. What comes about is phantasy-reality, something that can grow and develop lawfully out of divine, spiritual worlds into our own reality, the lawful possession, one can say, of the poor lad—modern man—limited as he is to the poverty of the outer sense world.

Of all the forms of literature the fairy tale is certainly least bound to outer reality. If we look at sagas, myths, and legends, we will find features in all of them that follow only supersensible laws, but these are actually immersed in the laws of external reality as they leave the spiritual and go into the outside world just as the source material, historical or history-related, is connected to a historical figure. Only the fairy tale does not allow itself to be manipulated around real figures; it stays quite free of them. It can use everything it finds of ordinary reality and has always used it. Therefore, it is the fairy tale that is the purest child of ancient, primitive clairvoyance; it is a sort of return payment for that early clairvoyance. Let old Sobersides, the pedant who never gets beyond his academic point of view, fail to perceive this. It doesn't matter; he needn't perceive it. The simple fact is that for every truth he hears, he asks, "Does it agree with reality?"

A person like Capesius is searching above everything else for truth. He finds no satisfaction in the question, "Does it agree with reality?" For he tells himself, "Is a matter of truth completely explained when you can say that it accords with the external world?" Things can really be true, and true and true again, as well as correct, and correct and ever correct, and still have as little relationship to reality as the truth of the little boy sent to buy rolls from the village baker. He figured out correctly that he would get five rolls for his ten kreuzers, but his figuring did not accord with reality; he practiced the same kind of thinking as the pedant who philosophizes about reality. You see, in that village, if you bought five rolls, you got an extra one thrown in—nothing to do with philosophy or logic, just plain reality.

In the same way Capesius is not interested in the question of how this or that idea or concept accords with reality. He asks first what the human soul perceives when it forms for itself a certain concept. The human soul, for one thing, perceives in mere external, everyday reality nothing more than emptiness, dryness, the tendency in itself continually to die. That is why Capesius so often needs the refreshment of Dame Felicia's fairy tales, needs exactly what is least true to outer reality but has substance that is real and is not necessarily true in the ordinary sense of the word. This substance of the fairy tale prepares him to find his way into the occult world.

In the fairy tale there is something left to us humans

that is like a grandchild of the clairvoyant experience of ancient human beings. It is within a form that is so lawful that no one who allows it to pour into his soul demands that its details accord with external reality. In fairy tale phantasy the poor boy, who has only a clever cat, has really also a palace obtruding directly into external reality. For every age, therefore, fairy tales can be a wonderful, spiritual nourishment. When we tell a child the *right* fairy tale, we enliven the child's soul so that it is led toward reality without always remaining glued to concepts true to everyday logic; such a relationship to reality dries up the soul and leaves it desolate. On the other hand, the soul can stay fresh and lively and able to penetrate the whole organism if, perceiving in the lawful figures of a fairy tale what is real in the highest sense of the word, it is lifted up far above the ordinary world. Stronger in life, comprehending life more vigorously, will be the person who in childhood has had fairy tales working their way into his soul.

For Capesius, fairy tales stimulate imaginative knowledge. What works and weaves from them into his soul is not their content, not their plot, but rather how they take their course, how one motif moves into the next. A motif may induce certain powers of soul to strive upward, a second motif persuades other powers to venture downward, still others will induce the soul forces to mingle and intertwine upward and downward. It is through this that Capesius' soul comes into active movement; out of his soul will then emerge what enables him finally to see into the spiritual world. For many people a fairy tale can be more stimulating than anything else. We will find in those that originated in earlier times motifs that show elements of ancient clairvoyance. The first tales did not begin by someone thinking them out; only the theories of modern professors of folklore explaining fairy tales begin like that. Fairy tales are never thought out; they are the final remains of ancient clairvoyance, experienced in dreams by human beings who still had that power. What was seen in a dream was told as a story —for instance, "Puss in Boots," one version of which I have just related. All the fairy tales in existence are thus the last remnants of that original clairvoyance. For this reason a genuine fairy tale can be created only when— consciously or unconsciously—an imagination is present in the soul of the teller, an imagination that projects itself into the soul. Otherwise, it is not a true fairy tale. Any sort of thought-out tale can never be genuine. Here and there today, when a real fairy tale is created, it arises only because an ardent longing has awakened in the writer toward those ancient times mankind lived through so long ago. The longing exists, although sometimes it creeps into such secret soul crevices that the writer fails to recognize in what he can create consciously how much is rising out of these hidden soul depths, and also how much is disfigured by what he creates out of his modern consciousness.

Here I should like to point out the following. Nothing put into poetic form can actually ever be grounded in truth unless it turns essentially to such a longing—a longing that has to be satisfied and that longs for the ancient clairvoyant penetration into the world, or unless it can use a new, genuine clairvoyance that does not need to reveal itself completely but can flash up in the hidden depths of the soul, casting only a many-hued shadow. This relationship still exists. How many people today still feel the necessity of rhyme? Where there is rhyme, how many people feel how necessary it is? Today there is that dreadful method of reciting poetry that suppresses the rhyme as far as possible and emphasizes the meaning, that is, whatever accords with external reality. But this element of poetry—rhyme—belongs to the stage of the development of language that existed at the time when the aftereffects of the ancient clairvoyance still prevailed.

Indeed, the end-rhyme belongs to the peculiar condition of soul expressing itself since man entered upon his modern development through the culture of the intellectual or feeling soul (*Verstandes- oder Gemütsseele*). Actually, the time in which the intellectual or feeling soul arose in men in the fourth post-Atlantean cultural epoch (747 B.C. to 1413 A.D.) is just the time when in poetry the memory dawned of earlier times that reach back into the ancient imaginative world. This dawning memory found its expression in the regular formation of the end-rhyme for what was lighting up in the intellectual or feeling soul; it was cultivated primarily by what developed in the fourth post-Atlantean epoch.

On the other hand, wherever the culture of the fourth epoch had penetrated, there was an incomparable refreshment through the effects of Christianity and the Mystery of Golgotha. It was this that poured into the European sentient soul. In the northern reaches of Europe the culture of the sentient soul had remained in a backward state, waiting for a higher stage, the intellectual soul culture that advanced from the Mediterranean and Southern Europe. This took place over the whole period of the fourth epoch and beyond, in order that what had developed in Central and Southern Europe, and in the Near East, could enter into the ancient sentient soul culture of Central Europe. There it could absorb the strength of will, the energy of will that comes to expression chiefly in the sentient soul culture. Thus we see the end-rhyme regularly at home in the poetry of the South,

94

and for the culture of the will that has already taken up Christianity, the other kind of rhyme—alliteration—as the appropriate mode of expression. In the alliterations of Northern and Central Europe we can feel the rolling, circling will pouring into the culture of the fourth epoch at its height, the culture of the intellectual or feeling soul.

It is astonishing that poets who want to bring to life, out of primeval soul forces in themselves, the memory of some primeval force in a particular sphere sometimes point back to the past in a quite haphazard fashion. This is the case with Wilhelm Jordan.[8] In his *Nibelungen* he wished to renew the ancient alliterations, and he achieved a remarkable effect as he wandered about like a bard, trying to resurrect the old mode of expression. People did not quite know what to make of it, because nowadays, in this intellectual time of ours, they think of speech as an expression only of meaning. People listen for the content of speech, not the effect that the sentient soul wants to obtain with alliteration, or that the intellectual soul wants to achieve with the end-rhyme. The consciousness soul really can no longer use any kind of rhyme; a poet today must find other devices.

Fräulein von Sivers [Marie Steiner] will now let us hear a short example of alliteration that will characterize how the artist, Wilhelm Jordan, wished to bring about the renewal of ancient modes.

Und es nahten die Nornen, von niemand gesehen,
Zu geräuschlosem Reigen und machten die Runde
Um diese Verlobten. Ein leiser Lufthauch,
Das war die Meinung der Minneberauschten,
Winde sich murmelnd herein zum Kamine;
Doch hinunter zur Nachtwelt, zu Nibelheims Tiefen,
Und hinauf zu den Wolken zu Walhalls Bewohnern

Erklang nun für andere als irdische Ohren
Vernehmlich wie Seesturm der Nornen Gesang:
Dein eigen ist alles,
Dein Heil wie dein Unheil,
Dein Wollen und Wähnen,
Dein Sinnen und Sein.
Wohl kommen, gekettet
In ewige Ordnung
Die Larven des Lebens,
Die Scharen des Scheins.
Sie ziehen die Zirkel,
Sie zeigen die Ziele,
Sie impfen den Abscheu,
Sie wecken den Wunsch;
Doch dein ist das Dünken,
Und wie du geworden,
So wirst du dich wenden,
Wir wissen die Wahl.

Rough English Translation

And the Norns then came nearer but no one could
    see them;
In soft silent steps they circled and swayed
Around the Betrothed—who, burning with love,
Thought a breath of sweet air was blowing about
    them;
While down to the night-world, in Nibelheim's
    nethermost,
And high in the heav'ns to the hosts of Valhalla
The Norns sang their song, for other than earth-ears
As clear as the clamorous raging of sea storms:
All is thine own:
Thy healing or hating,
Desires or delusions,

Thy thought and thy life.
Chained will come, cheerless,
In order eternal,
The hosts of the hidden,
The Larva of Life.
They mark out their measures,
They forecast fulfillment,
They implant raging passion,
Awaken the will.
Yet thine is the thinking,
The fashioning, forming,
The testing and turning:
We challenge thy choice.

Wilhelm Jordan really did bring the alliteration to life when he recited his poetry, but it is something that a modern person no longer can relate to completely. In order to agree sympathetically with what Jordan proposed as a kind of platform for his intentions,[9] one has to experience those ancient times imaginatively in those of the present. It is much like bringing to mind all the happenings of these last few days in our auditorium in the *Architektenhaus* during the Annual Meeting,[10] and perceiving them shrouded in astral currents that make visible what was spoken there. Then one can also discover that what in these days repeatedly played into our efforts for knowledge and understanding is the pictorial expression of a Jordan idea; that is, one could rightly understand what he set up as a kind of program to revive a mood that had held sway in the old Germanic world:

. . . der Sprache Springquell . . .
Bedarf nur der Leitung, um lauter und lieblich
Mit rauschendem Redestrom bis zum Rande
Der Vorzeit Gefässe wieder zu füllen

Und new zu verjüngen nach tausend Jahren
Die wundergewaltige uralte Weise
Der deutschen Dichtkunst.

(The source of speech requires only guidance to fill
again to the brim the ancient vessels with rushing
streams of verse, sonorous and beautiful; and after a
thousand years to bring anew to life the wonder
and the power of the ancient German art of poetry.)

But to attain this goal, an ear is needed that can perceive the sounds of speech. This belongs intrinsically to
the imaginations of the ancient clairvoyant epoch, for it
was then that the feeling for sounds originated. But what
is a speech sound? It is itself an imagination, an imaginative idea.

As long as you say *Licht* (light) and *Luft* (air) and can
think only of the brightness of the one and the wafting
movement of the other, you have not yet an imagination.
But the words themselves are imaginations. As soon as you
can feel their imaginative power, you will perceive in a
word like *Licht*, with the vowel sound "ee" predominat-
ing, a radiant, unbounded brightness; in *Luft*, with its
vowel sound "oo," a wholeness, an abundance. Because a
ray of light is a thin fullness and the air an abundant fullness, the alliterating "l" expresses the family relationship of
fullness. It is not unimportant whether you put together
words that alliterate, such as *Licht* and *Luft*, or do not
alliterate; it is not unimportant whether you string together the names of brothers or whether you put them
together in such a way that the hearer or reader feels that
cosmic will has brought them together, as in Gunther,
Gernot, Giselher. Such an ancient imagination the sentient soul could perceive in the alliteration.

In the end-rhyme the intellectual soul could recognize

98

itself as part of the ancient imagination. When language is made alive, its effects can be felt in the soul even into our dreams, where it can secrete certain imaginations for a person to become aware of in dream. These imaginations appear also to clairvoyance, correctly characterizing, for instance, the four elements. It does not always hold good, but if someone truly feels what, for example, *Licht* and *Luft* are, and lets this enter into a dream, there often blossoms out of the dream-fantasy something that can lead to a characterization of those elements, light and air. Human beings will not become aware of the secrets of language until it is led back to its origin, led back, in fact, to imaginative perception. Language actually originated in the time when man was not yet a "poor boy" but also when man had not yet a clever cat. In a way, he still lived attached to the Giant, Imagination, and out of the Giant's limbs he was aware of the audible imagination imbuing each sound. When a tone is laid hold of by the imagination, then the sound originates, the actual sound of speech.

These are the things I wanted to bring to you today, in a rather unpretentious and disconnected way, in order to show how we must bring to life again what mankind once lost but that has been rescued for our time. Just as Capesius wins his way to it, we must win it back, so that human beings can grow rightly into the era just ahead of us and find their way into higher worlds, thus truly to participate in them.

Translator's Notes

1. In the English translation of *The Portal of Initiation* these three sound distinctions could not be kept, except in the word "soul" at the end of Luna's speech, in which *the (spoken) diphthong* possesses a nuance of "u."
2. Rudolf Steiner, *Knowledge of the Higher Worlds and Its Attainment*, Anthroposophic Press, Inc., Spring Valley, NY, reprinted 1983.
3. Rudolf Steiner, *The Gospel of St. Matthew*, Rudolf Steiner Press, London, 1965.
4. Rudolf Steiner, *An Outline of Occult Science*, Anthroposophic Press, Inc., Spring Valley, NY, 1979.
5. Adolf Arenson (1855-1936) composed the music for the four Mystery Dramas at the request of Rudolf Steiner.
6. Rudolf Steiner, *The Wisdom of Man, of the Soul, and of the Spirit*, Anthroposophic Press, Inc., Spring Valley, NY, 1971.
7. Rudolf Steiner, *Inner Realities of Evolution*, Rudolf Steiner Press, London, 1953.
8. Wilhelm Jordan (1819-1904), *Nibelungen*, Canto One, *Sigfridsage*.
9. In the 1925 German edition of this lecture there is the following footnote: "Translated into the language of spiritual science, one could say that Jordan wished instinctively to revive for the consciousness soul as poetry what the sentient soul had earlier developed quite naturally."
10. December 10, 1911. Discussions took place on December 12, 14, 15.

www.ingramcontent.com/pod-product-compliance
Lightning Source LLC
LaVergne TN
LVHW091226080426
835509LV00009B/1191